Talk To Me In Korean
Workbook
Level 6

written by
Talk To Me In Korean

Talk To Me In Korean Workbook (Level 6)

1판 1쇄 · 1st edition published   2021. 7. 26.

1판 5쇄 · 5th edition published   2023. 10. 2.

지은이 · Written by   Talk To Me In Korean

책임편집 · Edited by   선경화 Kyung-hwa Sun, 석다혜 Dahye Seok, 김은희 Eunhee Kim

디자인 · Designed by   선윤아 Yoona Sun, 이은정 Eunjeong Lee

삽화 · Illustrations by   까나리 존스 Sungwon Jang

녹음 · Voice Recordings by   선경화 Kyung-hwa Sun

펴낸곳 · Published by   롱테일북스 Longtail Books

펴낸이 · Publisher   이수영 Su Young Lee

편집 · Copy-edited by   김보경 Florence Kim

주소 · Address   04033 서울특별시 마포구 양화로 113, 3층(서교동, 순흥빌딩)

    3rd Floor, 113 Yanghwa-ro, Mapo-gu, Seoul, KOREA

이메일 · E-mail   TTMIK@longtailbooks.co.kr

ISBN   979-11-91343-21-2 14710

*이 교재의 내용을 사전 허가 없이 전재하거나 복제할 경우 법적인 제재를 받게 됨을 알려 드립니다.

*잘못된 책은 구입하신 서점이나 본사에서 교환해 드립니다.

*정가는 표지에 표시되어 있습니다.

TTMIK - TALK TO ME IN KOREAN

Talk To Me In Korean Workbook
Level 6

Contents

How to Use
the Talk To Me In Korean Workbook

This workbook is designed to be used in conjunction with the Talk To Me In Korean Level 6 lessons, which are available as both a paperback book and an online course at https://talktomeinkorean.com. Developed by certified teachers to help you review and reinforce what you've learned, each lesson in this workbook contains five to seven activity sections chosen from five main review categories and 26 types of exercises.

Categories

1. Vocabulary
2. Comprehension
3. Dictation
4. Listening Comprehension
5. Speaking Practice

Types of Exercises

1. Matching
2. Translation Practice
3. Complete the Sentence
4. Complete the Dialogue
5. Dictation
6. Fill in the Blank
7. Multiple Choice
8. Listen & Repeat
9. Writing Practice
10. Correct/Incorrect

Starting from this Level 6 workbook, two listening categories are included as well: Dictation and Listening Comprehension. These listening categories are designed to aid in developing your Korean listening skills. After listening to the short dialogue between two or three people, answer the questions to check your understanding. Then practice speaking by repeating after the native speakers in the following Speaking Practice category. In order to get the most benefit from this category, please download the available audio files from https://talktomeinkorean.com/audio. The files are in MP3 format and are free of cost.

Lesson 1.
How about...?
어때요?

Section I - Vocabulary

Create a Korean phrase by matching one word on the left with the word that best fits with it from the right, and write it on the lines provided. Then choose the most accurate English translation from the Translation Bank and write it next to the Korean phrase. The first one has been done for you.

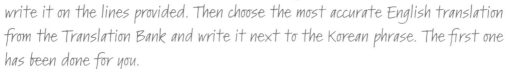

Translation Bank

to have lunch	to do it like this	to have an appointment
to go inside	to sit outside	to ask other people
to do again	to meet and talk about it tomorrow	

1. 점심을   하다

2. 안으로   있다

3. 이렇게   먹다

4. 다른 사람한테   앉다

5. 약속이   들어가다

6. 다시   물어보다

7. 밖에   만나서 이야기하다

8. 내일

1. 점심을 먹다 = to have lunch

   _____

2. _____

   _____

3. _____

   _____

4. _____

   _____

5. _____

   _____

6. _____

   _____

7. _____

   _____

8. _____

   _____

Section II - Translation Practice

Translate each sentence into Korean by combining a phrase
from Section I with "어때요?"

9. How about tomorrow? =

10. How about bibimbap? =

11. How about 5 o'clock? =

12. How about doing it this way? =

13. How about going inside? =

14. How about asking other people? =

15. How about meeting and talking about it tomorrow? =

Section III - Comprehension

Review: The topic marker -은/는 is added when you are comparing a number of items and have already asked about at least one. You can then ask about another by using -은/는 to say, "How about...?"

Choose one of the sentences that you made in Section II. Add the topic marker -은/는 in the correct place and complete the sentences/dialogues below.

16. 김치찌개 싫어요? 그럼 ～～～～～～～～～～～～～～～～～ ?

17. 2시에는 수업이 있는데, ～～～～～～～～～～～～～～～～ ?

18. 이 방법 별로예요? 그럼 ～～～～～～～～～～～～～～～～ ?

* 방법 = method, way

19. A: 오늘 같이 영화 볼까요?

   B: 오늘? 오늘은 약속 있는데, ～～～～～～～～～～～～～ ?

20. A: 날씨 좋으니까 밖에 앉을까요?

   B: 밖에 모기 많은데, ～～～～～～～～～～～～～～～ ?

* 모기 = mosquito

Section IV - Dictation

Listen to the sentences and fill in the blanks with the missing word or phrase. The sentences will be played twice.

21. 생일 선물로 〰〰〰〰〰〰〰〰〰〰〰〰〰〰〰〰〰〰〰〰〰〰〰〰 ?

22. 이렇게 〰〰〰〰〰〰〰〰〰〰〰〰〰〰〰〰〰〰〰〰〰〰〰〰〰 ?

Section V - Listening Comprehension

Listen to the dialogue and answer the following questions. The dialogue will be played twice.

23. Choose the topic of the conversation.

    a. Korean food

    b. What to eat for lunch

    c. The man's favorite restaurant

    d. The location of the restaurant

24. Choose the correct statement based on the dialogue.

    a. The food they like is different.

    b. The woman does not really like Korean food.

    c. The man knows of a restaurant that is famous for bibimbap.

    d. They will eat bibimbap for lunch.

Section VI - Speaking Practice

A native speaker will read the dialogue from Section V line by line. Listen and repeat each sentence one by one. You can check out the dialogue in the Answer Key at the back of the book.

Section I - Vocabulary

Match each Korean word or phrase to its common English translation. All words and phrases will be used in the following sections as well, so be sure to commit them to memory!

1. 생각하다

2. 유학 가다

3. 아이디어

4. 입고 가다

5. 어떻게

6. 이렇게

7. 소문

8. -에 대해서

a. about

b. how, in what manner

c. rumor

d. to think

e. to study abroad

f. idea

g. to go (somewhere) wearing (something)

h. like this

Section II - Comprehension

Answer the following multiple choice questions by circling the best answer.

9. Which Korean expression can have all of the following three meanings?

| How is it? | How about...? | What do you think? |

a. 어때요?

b. 어떤 것 같아요?

c. 어떻게 생각해요?

d. 제 아이디어 어때요?

10. Choose the question that does NOT have the meaning of, "What do you think?"

a. 어떻게 생각해요?

b. 어떤 생각 해요?

c. 어떤 것 같아요?

d. 어때요?

11. Which of the following can be used right after -에 대해서?

a. 어떤 것 같아요?

b. 어때요?

c. 어떻게 생각해요?

d. 어떤 생각 해요?

12. In order to use -에 대해서 after a verb, the verb first needs to be changed to the noun form. Which of the following is conjugated correctly and is ready to be combined with -에 대해서?

a. 이렇게 하다

b. 이렇게 하는

c. 이렇게 하기

d. 이렇게 하는 것

13. List the following expressions in order from most to least polite.

> 어떻게 생각해요?　　어떻게 생각하세요?　　어떤 것 같아?

    a. 어떻게 생각하세요?　어떻게 생각해요?　어떤 것 같아?

    b. 어떻게 생각해요?　어떻게 생각하세요?　어떤 것 같아?

    c. 어떤 것 같아?　어떻게 생각해요?　어떻게 생각하세요?

    d. 어떻게 생각해요?　어떤 것 같아?　어떻게 생각하세요?

Section III - Writing Practice

Make a sentence that includes all the phrases in the parentheses, plus one of the expressions meaning "What do you think about…?" that you learned in Talk To Me In Korean Level 6 Lesson 2.

> Ex) (학교, -ㄴ 것 같다, -아/어/여요?) ➝ 학교 어떤 것 같아요?

14. (제 아이디어, -에 대해서, -아/어/여요?)

    ➝

15. (그 소문, -에 대해서, -아/어/여?)

    ➝

16. (물어보다, -에 대해서, -(으)세요?)

    ➝

17. (회사, -ㄴ 것 같다, -아/어/여?)

    ➝

18. (이 옷 입고 가다, -ㄴ 것 같다, -아/어/여요?)

    ➝

19. (한국으로 유학 가다, -ㄴ 것 같다, -아/어/여요?)

→

Section IV - Dictation

Listen to the sentences and fill in the blanks with the missing word or phrase. The sentences will be played twice.

20. ~~~~~~ ?

21. 이 책 ~~~~~~~~~~~~~~~~~~~~~~~~~~~~~~~~~~~~~~~ ?

Section V - Listening Comprehension

22. Listen to the dialogue and mark which statements are correct and which are incorrect. The dialogue will be played twice.

* 결혼식 = wedding ceremony
* 화려하다 = to be colorful

a. The man is choosing what to wear to his friend's wedding.

b. The woman is choosing what to wear to Jooyeon's wedding.

c. The man thinks that his outfit is too colorful.

d. The woman thinks that her outfit is too colorful.

- Correct statements: ~~~~~~~~~~~~~~
- Incorrect statements: ~~~~~~~~~~~~~~

Section VI - Speaking Practice

A native speaker will read the dialogue from Section V line by line. Listen and repeat each sentence one by one. You can check out the dialogue in the Answer Key at the back of the book.

Lesson 3.
One of the most...

가장 ... 중의 하나

Section I - Vocabulary, Part 1

Let us review the vocabulary words from Talk To Me In Korean Level 6 Lesson 3.
Fill in the blanks by choosing the most appropriate word from the box.

들 중 의 가장 하나

1. 제일 = _____ = most

2. 가수 = singer, 가수_____ = singers

3. _____ = middle, center; among

4. _____ = of

5. _____, 둘, 셋 = one, two, three

Section II - Vocabulary, Part 2

Complete the phrases by choosing the most appropriate expression from the box and conjugating it correctly.

친하다   웹사이트   크다   제가 좋아하다   빠르다   카페   제가 자주 오다   방법   인기 있다

6. the singer who I like = ~~_____~~ 가수

7. close friend = ~~_____~~ 친구

8. popular movie = ~~_____~~ 영화

9. good cafe = 괜찮은 ~~_____~~

10. good method = 좋은 ~~_____~~

11. good website = 좋은 ~~_____~~

12. the place that I come to often = ~~_____~~ 곳

13. fast way/path = ~~_____~~ 길

14. big reason = ~~_____~~ 이유

Section III - Conjugation Practice

Complete the sentences by using the phrases from Section II.

[For questions 6a to 8a, please use both -들 and -의.]

6a. ~~_____~~ 이에요.
    = He/she is one of the singers that I like the most.

7a. ~~_____~~ 이에요.
    = He/she is one of my closest friends.

8a. ＿＿＿＿＿＿＿＿＿＿＿＿＿＿＿＿＿＿＿＿ 예요.

 = It is one of the most popular movies.

[For questions 9a to 11a, please use -의 only. Do not use -들.]

9a. ＿＿＿＿＿＿＿＿＿＿＿＿＿＿＿＿＿＿ 이에요.

 = It is one of the best cafes.

10a. ＿＿＿＿＿＿＿＿＿＿＿＿＿＿＿＿＿＿＿ 예요.

 = It is one of the best methods.

11a. ＿＿＿＿＿＿＿＿＿＿＿＿＿＿＿＿＿＿＿ 예요.

 = It is one of the best websites.

[For questions 12a to 14a, do not use -들 or -의.]

12a. ＿＿＿＿＿＿＿＿＿＿＿＿＿＿＿＿＿＿＿ 예요.

 = It is one of the places that I come to most often.

13a. ＿＿＿＿＿＿＿＿＿＿＿＿＿＿＿＿＿＿＿ 예요.

 = It is one of the fastest ways/paths.

14a. ＿＿＿＿＿＿＿＿＿＿＿＿＿＿＿＿＿＿＿ 예요.

 = It is one of the biggest reasons.

Section IV - Dictation

Listen to the sentences and fill in the blanks with the missing word or phrase. The sentences will be played twice.

15. _____ 예요.

16. 제가 _____ 예요.

Section V - Listening Comprehension

17. Listen to the dialogue and choose the correct statement. The dialogue will be played twice.

* 박사 과정 = PhD
* 등록금 = tuition

a. The man is thinking of giving up on his PhD.

b. The man and the woman are attending the same graduate school.

c. The only reason why the man is thinking of giving up on his PhD is the cost of tuition.

d. One of the reasons why the man chose his PhD program was the cost of tuition.

Section VI - Speaking Practice

A native speaker will read the dialogue from Section V line by line. Listen and repeat each sentence one by one. You can check out the dialogue in the Answer Key at the back of the book.

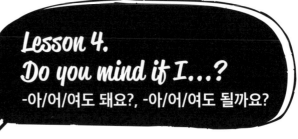

Lesson 4.
Do you mind if I...?
-아/어/여도 돼요?, -아/어/여도 될까요?

Section I - Vocabulary

Complete the sentences by choosing the most appropriate word from the box and adding -(으)ㄹ게요 or -아/어/여 주세요.

열다	닫다	기다리다	설명하다
먼저 가다	열어 보다	나갔다가 오다	나중에 전화하다

1. 창문 좀 ＿＿＿＿＿＿＿＿게요. = I will open the window.

2. ＿＿＿＿＿＿＿＿게요. = I will call you later.

3. 저 ＿＿＿＿＿＿＿＿게요. = I will leave first.

4. 이거 ＿＿＿＿＿＿＿＿게요. = I will try opening this.

5. 창문 ＿＿＿＿＿＿＿＿게요. = I will close the window.

6. 잠깐 ＿＿＿＿＿＿＿＿게요. = I will go somewhere and come back in a moment.

7. 조금만 ＿＿＿＿＿＿＿＿주세요. = Please wait for a bit.

8. 한 번 더 ＿＿＿＿＿＿＿＿주세요. = Please explain one more time.

Talk To Me In Korean Workbook

Section II - Conjugation Practice

Rewrite all of the sentences from Section I on the lines below after replacing the endings in the Section I sentences with the endings in the parentheses below. The sentence endings below are all different ways to ask, "Do you mind…?"

1a.

(-아/어/여도 돼요?) ⁓⁓⁓⁓⁓⁓⁓⁓⁓⁓⁓⁓⁓⁓⁓⁓⁓⁓⁓⁓

2a.

(-아/어/여도 돼요?) ⁓⁓⁓⁓⁓⁓⁓⁓⁓⁓⁓⁓⁓⁓⁓⁓⁓⁓⁓

3a.

(-아/어/여도 괜찮아요?) ⁓⁓⁓⁓⁓⁓⁓⁓⁓⁓⁓⁓⁓⁓⁓⁓⁓

4a.

(-아/어/여도 괜찮아요?) ⁓⁓⁓⁓⁓⁓⁓⁓⁓⁓⁓⁓⁓⁓⁓⁓⁓

5a.

(-아/어/여도 될까요?) ⁓⁓⁓⁓⁓⁓⁓⁓⁓⁓⁓⁓⁓⁓⁓⁓⁓⁓

6a.

(-아/어/여도 될까요?) ⁓⁓⁓⁓⁓⁓⁓⁓⁓⁓⁓⁓⁓⁓⁓⁓⁓⁓

7a.

(-아/어/여 주실래요?) ⁓⁓⁓⁓⁓⁓⁓⁓⁓⁓⁓⁓⁓⁓⁓⁓⁓

8a.

(-아/어/여 주실래요?) ⁓⁓⁓⁓⁓⁓⁓⁓⁓⁓⁓⁓⁓⁓⁓⁓⁓

Section III - Comprehension

Complete the dialogues below by choosing one of the sentences from Section II. Use either polite or casual form, depending on the context of the dialogue.

9. A: 다혜야, 좀 더운데 ＿＿＿＿＿＿＿＿＿＿＿＿＿＿＿?
    B: 응.

10. A: 여보세요.
    B: 경화야!
    A: 승완아, 나 지금 회의 들어가야 되는데 내가 ＿＿＿＿＿＿＿＿＿?

11. A: 준비 다 했어?
    B: 거의 다 했는데 ＿＿＿＿＿＿＿＿＿＿＿＿?
    A: 빨리 해.

12. A: 질문 있어요?
    B: 선생님, 이 문법 너무 어려운데 ＿＿＿＿＿＿＿＿＿?

13. A: 정말 죄송한데, 저 ＿＿＿＿＿＿＿＿＿? 급한 전화가 와서요.
    B: 아, 네.

    * 급한 전화 = urgent phone call

Section IV - Dictation

Listen to the sentences and fill in the blanks with the missing word or phrase. The sentences will be played twice.

14. 내일 ＿＿＿＿＿＿＿＿＿＿＿＿＿＿＿?

15. 여기 ＿＿＿＿＿＿＿＿＿＿＿＿＿＿＿?

Section V - Listening Comprehension

Listen to the dialogue and answer the following questions. The dialogue will be played twice.

16. Where is this conversation taking place?

    a. 식당   *b.* 핸드폰 가게   *c.* 사무실   *d.* 여자의 집

17. What will the man do after the conversation is finished?

    a. 안으로 들어간다.

    b. 전화번호를 쓴다.

    c. 여자에게 전화한다.

    d. 빈자리가 있는지 물어본다.   * 빈자리 = empty seat

Section VI - Speaking Practice

A native speaker will read the dialogue from Section V line by line. Listen and repeat each sentence one by one. You can check out the dialogue in the Answer Key at the back of the book.

Lesson 5.
I am in the middle of -ing
-고 있는 중이에요, -는 중이에요

Section I - Vocabulary

Fill in the blanks by using the words and phrases from the box. The first one has been done for you.

찾다	밥 먹다	공부하다	일하다	
운동하다	요리하다	회사에 가다	숙제하다	하다

1. 열쇠를 찾고 있어요. = I am looking for the key.

2. _____ 고 있어요. = I am going to the office.

3. _____ 고 있어요. = I am exercising.

4. _____ 고 있어요. = I am cooking.

5. _____ 고 있었어요. = I was studying.

6. _____ 고 있었어요. = I was eating a meal.

7. 뭐 _____ 고 있었어요? = What are you doing now?

8. _____ 고 있을 거예요. = I will be working.

9. _____ 고 있어요. = I am doing my homework.

Section II - Conjugation Practice

Rewrite the Korean sentences from Section I – Vocabulary. Add -는 중 to emphasize the fact that you are doing something right at this very moment.

1a. _____

2a. _____

3a. _____

4a. _____

5a. _____

6a. _____

7a. _____

8a. _____

9a. _____

Section III - Complete the Sentence

Complete the sentences by conjugating the words in the parentheses, then translate them into your preferred language. (Translations in the Answer Key are given in English.)

10. _____, 나중에 _____
(회의하다 + -는 중이다 + -(으)ㄴ데)   (전화하다 + -아/어/여도 될까요?)

=

11. 아직 _____, 조금만 _____
(고르다 + -는 중이다 + -(으)ㄴ데)   (기다리다 + -아/어/여 줄래요?)

=

12. 지금 _____, 음악 소리 좀 _____
(공부하다 + -는 중이다 + -(으)ㄴ데)   (줄이다 + -아/어/여 줄래요?)

=

* 줄이다 = to turn down

13. 지금 _____, 문자 메시지로 _____
(운전하다 + -는 중이다 + -(으)ㄴ데)   (보내다 + -아/어/여 주시겠어요?)

=

14. _____, 좀 늦을 것 같으니까 먼저 _____
(가다 + -는 중이다 + -(으)ㄴ데)   (시작하다 + -(으)세요)

=

Section IV - Dictation

Listen to the sentences and fill in the blanks with the missing word or phrase. The sentences will be played twice.

15. 뭐 하 ~~_____~~ ?

16. ~~_____~~ .

Section V - Listening Comprehension

17. Listen to the dialogue and choose the correct statement. The dialogue will be played twice.

    a. The man is on his way to work in the morning.

    b. The man is almost home now.

    c. The man does not have his wallet at the moment.

    d. The man is late for work because he is looking for his car keys now.

Section VI - Speaking Practice

A native speaker will read the dialogue from Section V line by line. Listen and repeat each sentence one by one. You can check out the dialogue in the Answer Key at the back of the book.

Lesson 6.
Word Builder #9   -님

Section I - Vocabulary

Review the vocabulary words for job titles from Talk To Me In Korean Level 6 Lesson 6. Fill in the chart with each profession's official job title and term of address.

	Official Job Title	How to Address Them
1. teacher		
2. doctor		
3. professor		
4. head of a company		
5. head of the department (or manager)		
6. section chief		
7. dean or president of a college		

Section II - Comprehension

Answer the following questions by choosing the most appropriate word from the box.

8. The term 님 has basically the same function as 씨, but one is much more formal and polite than the other. Which expression sounds more formal and polite when used to address Kyung-hwa?

> 경화 씨   경화 님

9. Which word is used to call your mother in a formal and polite way?

> 엄마   어머니   어머님

10. Choose the term you can use when referring to someone else's father in a polite way.

> 아빠   아버지   아버님

11. Choose the word that best fills in the blank.

> 엄마   어머니   어머님

저희 _____ (이)세요. = She is my husband's mother.

12. Which term do men use when addressing an older woman in a polite way?

> 누님   형님

13. How do you say "I am a doctor" in Korean? Choose one word from the box and write it in a full sentence.

> 의사   선생님   의사 선생님

Answer: _____.

14. In a business-related context, how do you address your 손님?

> 손   고객   고객님

15. Using the words in the box, complete the pyramid that shows the general Korean corporate titles and hierarchy.

> 부장   과장   사장

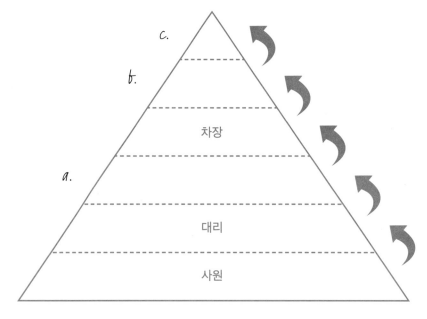

* 사원 = employee / 대리 = deputy section chief /
차장 = deputy head of a department

Section III - Dictation

Listen to the sentences and fill in the blanks with the missing word or phrase. The sentences will be played twice.

16. 선현우 ꠏꠏꠏꠏꠏꠏꠏꠏꠏꠏꠏꠏ, 들어오세요.

17. ꠏꠏꠏꠏꠏꠏꠏꠏꠏꠏꠏꠏ, 안녕하세요?

18. ꠏꠏꠏꠏꠏꠏꠏꠏꠏꠏꠏꠏ, ꠏꠏꠏꠏꠏꠏꠏꠏꠏꠏꠏꠏ께서 찾으세요.

Section IV - Listening Comprehension

Listen to the dialogue and answer the following question. The dialogue will be played twice.

19. Who is having this conversation?

    a. Minsong and her mother

    b. Minsong and her teacher

    c. Minsong's teacher and Minsong's mother

    d. Minsong's teacher and the teacher's mother

Section V - Speaking Practice

A native speaker will read the dialogue from Section IV line by line. Listen and repeat each sentence one by one. You can check out the dialogue in the Answer Key at the back of the book.

Lesson 7.
One way or another
어차피

Section I - Vocabulary

Answer the following multiple choice questions by circling the best answer(s).

1. Which of the following is the adverb form of "재미있다 (= to be fun)"?

   a. 재미있고   b. 재미있네   c. 재미있는   d. 재미있게

2. Choose the pair of words that are NOT antonyms.

   a. 오다 ↔ 가다

   b. 늦다 ↔ 늦게

   c. 빨리 ↔ 천천히

   d. 출근하다 ↔ 퇴근하다

3. Choose the pair of words that can fit in the blanks.

   - 안 입는 옷을 _____ ㉠ _____
     = to throw away the clothes that one does not wear

   - 사무실에 _____ ㉡ _____
     = to stop by one's office

   a. ㉠ 버리다   ㉡ 들르다   b. ㉠ 들르다   ㉡ 버리다

   c. ㉠ 가져가다   ㉡ 들어가다   d. ㉠ 들어가다   ㉡ 가져가다

4. "가지다 (= to have)" and "가다 (= to go)" can be combined to create the verb 가져가다. What does 가져가다 mean?

    a. to bring, to take

    b. to prepare

    c. package

    d. thief, burglar

5. Read the following dialogue and then choose the correct meaning of the phrase 연락 오다.

> 경은: 현우 씨한테 연락 왔어요?
>
> 주연: 아니요. 연락이 없네요.
>
> 경은: 제가 연락해 볼게요. 현우 씨 전화번호가 뭐였죠?

    a. to stay in touch

    b. to hear from someone

    c. to lose touch with someone

    d. cannot reach, cannot contact

6. Choose the adverb that fits correctly in the blank.

> _____ 사무실에 오다 = to come to the office in a little bit

    a. 거의

    b. 다시

    c. 이따가

    d. 어차피

7. What is the correct translation of the Korean word 어차피? Circle all correct answers.

a. anyway

b. one way or another

c. not even... to begin with

d. in any case

e. after all

Did you answer all the questions? All words in this section are used in the following sections as well, so be sure to check out the answers and commit them to memory before you move on to the next section!

Section II - Complete the Dialogue

Fill in the blanks by taking a sentence fragment from column A and matching it with the most appropriate fragment from column B. Each fragment is used only once.

A	B
어차피 늦었으니까	연락 안 와요
어차피 아무한테도	오지 마세요
어차피 작아져서	버리려고 했어요
어차피 거의 다 마셔서	못 할 것 같네요
어차피 오늘 다	못 입어요
어차피 해야 하는 일이니까	재미있게 해요

8. A: 다혜 씨, 미안해요. 저 지금 가는 중이에요. 빨리 갈게요.

B: _____.

9. A: 핸드폰 안 가져가요?

    B: 네. ～～～～～～～～～～～～～～～～～～～～～～～～～～～～～～～～～～ .

10. A: 이렇게 좋은 옷을 버려요? 아깝다.   * 아깝다 = *to be too good to throw away*

    B: ～～～～～～～～～～～～～～～～～～～～～～～～～～～～～～～～～～～～ .

11. A: 숙제하기 너무 싫어요.

    B: ～～～～～～～～～～～～～～～～～～～～～～～～～～～～～～～～～～～～ .

12. A: 우리 내일 다시 만나서 하는 게 어때요?

    B: 그래요. ～～～～～～～～～～～～～～～～～～～～～～～～～～～～～～～～ .

13. A: 제 책상 위에 커피 있었는데... 혹시 승완 씨가 버렸어요?

    B: 네. 마시려고 했어요? 미안해요.

    A: 아니에요. 괜찮아요. ～～～～～～～～～～～～～～～～～～～～～～～～ .

Section III - Dictation

Listen to the sentences and fill in the blanks with the missing word or phrase.
The sentences will be played twice.

14. ～～～～～～～～～～～～～～～～～～～～～～～～ 못 해요.

15. ～～～～～～～～～～～～～～～～～～～～～～～～～～～～～～～～～ 아니에요.

Section IV – Listening Comprehension

Listen to the dialogue and answer the following questions. The dialogue will be played twice.

16. Where is this conversation taking place?

    a. In Seokjin's room

    b. At the library

    c. In the classroom

    d. In the office

17. Why is Seokjin not taking his bag? Write the reason in Korean using 어차피.

    Answer: _____ 니까.

Section V – Speaking Practice

A native speaker will read the dialogue from Section IV line by line. Listen and repeat each sentence one by one. You can check out the dialogue in the Answer Key at the back of the book.

Lesson 8. -(으)ㄴ/는지 잘 모르겠어요
I'm not sure if...

Section I - Vocabulary

Please define/translate each word and write it in your preferred language below. (Translations in the Answer Key are given in English.)

1. 맞다 =

2. 끝나다 =

3. 열다 =

4. 크다 =

5. 있다 =

6. 어디 =

7. 책 =

8. 서점 =

9. 뜻 =

10. 모르다 =

Section II - Conjugation Practice

Fill in the chart. The first one has been done for you.

Word/Expression in Infinitive Form	+ -(으)ㄴ/는지	+ -았/었/였는지	+ -(으)ㄹ지
11. 맞다	맞는지	맞았는지	맞을지
12. 끝나다			
13. 열다			
14. 크다			
15. 있다			
16. 어디이다			
17. 책이다			
18. 서점이다			
19. 뜻이다			
20. 모르다			

Section III - Translation Practice

Translate each sentence into Korean using –지 잘 모르겠어요.

21. I am not sure if it is good. =

22. I am not sure if this is the right place. =

23. I am not sure who he is. =

24. I am not sure if the bookstore is open. =

25. I am not sure where I have to buy it. =

26. I am not sure what I will have to do. =

27. I am not sure when it will be finished. =

Section IV - Fill in the Blank

Make sure to include the "or not" meaning as contained in "whether or not".

28. 내일 _____ 잘 모르겠어요.

= I am not sure whether or not we will meet tomorrow.

29. 휴가를 _____ 잘 모르겠어요.

= I am not sure whether or not to go on vacation.

30. _____ 잘 모르겠어요.

= I am not sure whether or not it was over.

31. 오늘 문을 _____ 잘 모르겠어요.

= I am not sure whether or not it is open.

32. 집에 우유가 ＿＿＿＿＿＿＿＿＿＿＿＿＿＿ 잘 모르겠어요.

= I am not sure whether or not there is milk at home.

Section V - Dictation

Listen to the sentences and fill in the blanks with the missing word or phrase. The sentences will be played twice.

33. 저도 이 식당 처음 와 봐서 ＿＿＿＿＿＿＿＿＿＿＿.

34. 현우 씨가 요즘 바빠서 ＿＿＿＿＿＿＿＿＿＿＿.

Section VI - Listening Comprehension

True/False - Listen to the dialogue and decide if the statement is true or false. Write "T" if the statement is true and "F" if it is false. The dialogue will be played twice.

35. They are in the yoga studio now. ＿＿＿

36. They are having a conversation right after their yoga class. ＿＿＿

37. Kyung-hwa thinks that yoga is one of the best exercises. ＿＿＿

38. Kyung-hwa is not sure if yoga is good. ＿＿＿

Section VII - Speaking Practice

A native speaker will read the dialogue from Section VI line by line. Listen and repeat each sentence one by one. You can check out the dialogue in the Answer Key at the back of the book.

Lesson 9. -(으)니/는 김에
While you are at it

Section I - Vocabulary

Circle the correct translation of the Korean expression.

1. 나가다   a. to go inside   b. to go outside

2. 들어가다   a. to go inside   b. to go outside

3. 시작하다   a. to start, to begin   b. to be over, to be finished

4. 끝나다   a. to start, to begin   b. to be over, to be finished

5. 빌리다   a. to borrow   b. to return

6. 반납하다   a. to borrow   b. to return

7. 부탁하다   a. to ask for a favor   b. to do a favor

8. 부탁을 들어주다 a. to ask for a favor   b. to do a favor

Section II - Complete the Sentence

Complete the sentences by conjugating the words in the parentheses, then translate them into your preferred language. (Translations in the Answer Key are given
in English.)

9. 백화점에 ＿＿＿＿＿＿＿＿＿ 서점에도 잠깐 ＿＿＿＿＿＿＿＿＿＿＿?
   （가다 + -는 김에）   （들르다 + -(으)ㄹ까）

   =   * 들르다 = to stop by

10. 그 책 ＿＿＿＿＿＿＿＿＿ 이 책도 ＿＿＿＿＿＿＿＿＿＿＿.
    （반납하다 + -는 김에）   （반납하다 + -아/어/여 주세요）

    =

11. 밖에 ＿＿＿＿＿＿＿＿＿ 제 부탁 하나만 ＿＿＿＿＿＿＿＿＿.
    （나가다 + -ㄴ 김에）   （들어주다 + -(으)세요）

    =

12. 서울에 ＿＿＿＿＿＿＿＿＿ 석진 씨한테 ＿＿＿＿＿＿＿＿＿?
    （오다 + -ㄴ 김에）   （연락해 보다 + -(으)ㄹ까요）

    =

13. ＿＿＿＿＿＿＿＿＿ 끝까지 ＿＿＿＿＿＿＿＿＿＿＿!
    （시작하다 + -ㄴ 김에）   （해 보다 + -(으)려고 해요）

    =

Section III - Complete the Dialogue

Read each dialogue and circle the correct answer.

14. A: 도서관 가요?

    B: 네.

    A: 그럼 <u>가는 김에</u> / <u>간 김에</u> 제 책도 반납해 주세요.

15. A: 지금 어디예요?

    B: 도서관이에요.

    A: 오, 그럼 도서관 <u>가는 김에</u> / <u>간 김에</u> Talk To Me In Korean Level 6 책 좀

    빌려다 주세요.   * 빌려다 주다 = to borrow something for someone

16. A: 우리 언제 같이 밥 먹어요.

    B: <u>말이 나오는 김에</u> / <u>말이 나온 김에</u> 오늘 먹을까요?

17. A: 현우 씨 사무실이 이 근처에 있다고 했는데…

    B: 그래요? 그럼 여기 <u>오는 김에</u> / <u>온 김에</u> 현우 씨한테 연락해 볼까요?

                                          * 근처 = near, nearby

18. A: 우리 <u>나오는 김에</u> / <u>나온 김에</u> 점심 먹고 들어갈까요?

    B: 좋아요. 제가 경은 씨한테 점심 먹고 간다고 문자 보낼게요.

19. A: <u>파마하는 김에</u> / <u>파마한 김에</u> 염색도 하는 게 어때요?

    B: 시간이 없어서 오늘은 파마만 할게요.

                                    * 파마하다 = to have one's hair permed
                                    * 염색하다 = to have one's hair colored

20. A: 세탁기 돌리려고 하는데, <u>돌리는 김에</u> / <u>돌린 김에</u> 이 옷도 같이 빨아 줄까요?

    B: 네. 고마워요.   * 세탁기(를) 돌리다 = to run the washing machine

Section IV - Dictation

Listen to the sentences and fill in the blanks with the missing word or phrase. The sentences will be played twice.

21. _____ 하나만 더 할게요.

22. _____ 이 책 좀 _____ 주세요.

Section V - Listening Comprehension

Listen to the dialogue and answer the following question. The dialogue will be played twice.

23. What is the woman most likely to say next after this dialogue?

* 끓이다 = to boil

a. 맛있었어?

b. 라면 먹는 중이었어?

c. 말 나온 김에 우리 라면 먹을까?

d. 그래? 그럼 끓이는 김에 내 것도 부탁해.

Section VI - Speaking Practice

A native speaker will read the dialogue from Section V line by line. Listen and repeat each sentence one by one. You can check out the dialogue in the Answer Key at the back of the book.

Lesson 10.
Sentence Building Drill #6

Section I - Vocabulary

Read the dialogue below and then fill in the blanks by choosing the correct word from the box and conjugating it properly. Each word is used only once.

| 자주 | 이따가 | 나중에 | 친하다 | 들르다 | 통화하다 | 가져가다 |

A: 졸업식 때 찍은 사진이네요.

B: 네.

A: 이 친구들 중에서 누구랑 제일 1. _____ 어요?

B: 이 친구요. 이름이 경화예요.

A: 그렇구나. 졸업한 후에도 2. _____ 연락해요?

B: 그럼요. 경화랑 거의 매일 3. _____ . 아, 4. _____

저녁에 경화 만나는데, 같이 만날래요?

A: 아, 저 오늘 약속 있어요.

B: 그래요? 그럼 5. _____ 같이 만나요.

A: 좋아요. 벌써 나가요?

B: 네. 경화 만나기 전에 서점에 잠깐 6. _____ 려고요.

A: 밖에 비 오니까 우산 7. _____ 세요.

B: 네. 고마워요.

Section II - Complete the Sentence

Fill in the blanks using the words in the parentheses. Make sure to arrange them in the correct order.

8. (중, 지금, 일하는)

저 _____ 이어서 전화 못 받아요.

9. (중, 지금, 통화하는)

주연 씨 _____ 이에요.

10. (가도, 늦을, 어차피)

_____ 지금 _____ 것 같아요.

11. (못, 다, 할, 어차피)

_____ 오늘 _____ 것 같아요.

12. (제일, 친구, 친한, 중, 한, 명)

저랑 _____ 이에요.

13. (제일, 카페, 자주, 가는, 중, 한, 곳)

여기가 제가 ＿＿＿＿＿＿＿＿＿＿＿＿＿＿＿＿＿＿＿ 이에요.

Section III - Sentence Extension

Complete the sentences by choosing the appropriate sentence from Section II and conjugating it with -(으)ㄴ/는데 or -(으)니까 below.

Ex) 친구들 만날 거예요. + -(으)ㄴ/는데 + 같이 갈래요?

➝ 친구들 만날 건데, 같이 갈래요?

(= I'm going to meet my friends. Do you want to join?)

14. ＿＿＿＿＿＿＿＿＿＿＿＿＿＿＿＿, 같이 가 볼래요?

15. ＿＿＿＿＿＿＿＿＿＿＿＿＿＿＿＿, 만나 볼래요?

16. ＿＿＿＿＿＿＿＿＿＿＿＿＿＿＿＿, 가지 말까요?

17. ＿＿＿＿＿＿＿＿＿＿＿＿＿＿＿＿, 내일 다시 만나서 할까요?

Ex) 오늘 바빠요. + -(으)니까 + 내일 만나요.

➝ 오늘 바쁘니까 내일 만나요.

(= I'm busy today, so let's meet tomorrow.)

18. ＿＿＿＿＿＿＿＿＿＿＿＿＿＿＿＿, 나중에 전화할게요.

19. ＿＿＿＿＿＿＿＿＿＿＿＿＿＿＿＿, 이따가 전화하라고 할게요.

Section IV – Dictation

Listen to the sentences and fill in the blanks with the missing word or phrase. The sentences will be played twice.

20. _____ 이었어요.

21. 제가 _____ 인데, 같이 볼래요?

Section V – Listening Comprehension

22. Listen to the dialogue and choose the correct statement. The dialogue will be played twice.

    a. The man is in the middle of playing a game.

    b. The man is playing a game while eating snacks.

    c. The woman is playing a game with the man.

    d. It was the first time for the woman to try Korean snacks.

Section VI – Speaking Practice

A native speaker will read the dialogue from Section V line by line. Listen and repeat each sentence one by one. You can check out the dialogue in the Answer Key at the back of the book.

Section I - Vocabulary

Match each Korean word to its common English translation.

1. 의미하다

a. so...; you mean...; I mean...

2. 뜻

b. already

3. 제

c. by oneself

4. 그러니까

d. to mean, to imply

5. 벌써

e. the best

6. 혼자

f. my (honorific)

7. 진심

g. real, really

8. 최고

h. meaning

9. 진짜

i. one's whole heart, sincerity

Section II - Writing Practice

Write each sentence using the following structure with the words given in the parentheses. An example has been provided.

> Structure:
>
> 그러니까 제 말은... -(이)라는/다는 말이에요. = (So) I mean...
>
> Example: (현우 씨, 제일, 바쁘다)
> 그러니까 제 말은 현우 씨가 제일 바쁘다는 말이에요.
> = I mean, Hyunwoo is the busiest.

10. (벌써, 다, 끝나다)

_____.

= I mean, it is already over.

11. (지난주, 이미, 사다)

_____.

= I mean, I already bought it last week.

12. (경은 씨, 최고)

_____.

= I mean, Kyeong-eun is the best.

13. (주연 씨, 정말, 사랑하다)

_____.

= I mean, I really love Jooyeon.

14. (아직, 고르는 중이다)

~~~~~~ .

= I mean, I am still in the middle of choosing.

Section III - Comprehension

Decide if the Korean sentence is correct (O) or incorrect (X). If it is incorrect,
write the full sentence correctly below.

15. 그 책을 벌써 다 읽었다고요? (O / X)

= You mean, you already finished reading the book?

↣

16. 아이스크림이 먹고 싶라고요. (O / X)

= I mean, I want to eat ice cream.

↣

17. 제일 자주 가는 카페다고요. (O / X)

= I mean, it is the cafe I go to most often.

↣

18. 그러니까 제 말은 언젠가 가고 싶다는 말이에요. (O / X)

= So, I mean, I want to go someday.

↣

19. 다음 주 금요일에, 아니, 토요일에 올 거예요. (O / X)

= It will come next Friday, I mean, Saturday.

↣

20. 그러니까 제 말은 지금 아무것도 안 하고 있다라는 말이에요. (O / X)

= So, I mean, I am not doing anything now.

↣

Section IV - Dictation

Listen to the sentences and fill in the blanks with the missing word or phrase. The sentences will be played twice.

21. 그러니까 _____?

22. 그러니까 _____?

Section V - Listening Comprehension

Listen to the dialogue and answer the following questions. The dialogue will be played twice.

* 화려하다 = to be colorful, to be bright

23. Choose the correct statement according to the dialogue.

a. The woman likes the color of the sneakers suggested by the man.

b. The woman likes the style of the sneakers suggested by the man.

c. The woman is going to buy the sneakers suggested by the man.

d. The woman is going to buy the sneakers for the man.

24. Choose the sentence that is different from what the woman implied at the end of the dialogue.

a. 그러니까 싫다는 말이에요.

b. 그러니까 다른 색깔도 보고 싶다는 말이에요.

c. 그러니까 색깔이 너무 화려하다는 말이에요.

d. 그러니까 운동화 말고 다른 신발이 좋다는 말이에요.

Section VI - Speaking Practice

A native speaker will read the dialogue from Section V line by line. Listen and repeat each sentence one by one. You can check out the dialogue in the Answer Key at the back of the book.

Section I - Vocabulary

Answer the following multiple choice questions by circling the best answer.

1. Which word is the same as 무엇?

    a. 뭐   b. 무슨   c. 뭔   d. 무얼

2. Which of the following is the modifying form of 무엇?

    a. 무얼   b. 뭐게   c. 무슨   d. 무게

3. Which of the following is short for 그것이?

    a. 그건   b. 그게   c. 그거   d. 그걸

4. Choose the set of words that can fill in the blanks.

    • _____ ㉠ _____ 가 들려요. = I can hear the sound.
    • _____ ㉡ _____ 드릴게요. = I will tell you.

    a. ㉠ 소리   ㉡ 말   b. ㉠ 음악   ㉡ 말씀
    c. ㉠ 음악   ㉡ 말   d. ㉠ 소리   ㉡ 말씀

5. Choose the adverb that best fits in the blank.

    _____ 조용해졌어요. = It became quiet all of a sudden.

    a. 갑자기   b. 계속   c. 천천히   d. 빠르게

6. 그만하다 means "to stop" in English. What is the correct translation of the Korean word 그만두다?

   a. to try

   b. to quit

   c. to realize

   d. to experience

Section II - Comprehension

Answer the following multiple choice questions by circling the best answer.

7. Choose the answer that CANNOT be the meaning of all three expressions.

무슨 말이에요?　　무슨 소리예요?　　무슨 말씀이세요?

   a. What do you mean?

   b. What is this sound?

   c. What does that mean?

   d. What are you talking about?

8. Choose the word that does NOT form the sentence, "What do you mean?" when used in the blank.

무슨 ＿＿＿＿＿ 예요/이에요?

   a. 소리   b. 말   c. 뜻   d. 일

9. List the following expressions from least to most polite.

무슨 말씀이세요?　　무슨 소리예요?　　무슨 말이에요?

a. 무슨 소리예요? - 무슨 말이에요? - 무슨 말씀이세요?

b. 무슨 말이에요? - 무슨 소리예요? - 무슨 말씀이세요?

c. 무슨 말씀이세요? - 무슨 말이에요? - 무슨 소리예요?

d. 무슨 소리예요? - 무슨 말씀이세요? - 무슨 말이에요?

10. Which expression CANNOT fit in the blank?

> A: 승완 씨는 오늘 안 왔어요?
>
> B: 승완 씨 지난주에 학교 그만뒀어요.
>
> A: 네? 그게 _____? 아무 이야기도 없었는데...

a. 무슨 소리예요   b. 무슨 말이에요   c. 무슨 뜻이에요

11. Choose the expression you can use when you do not understand someone's comment or point very well.

a. 무슨 말인지 잘 알겠어요.   b. 무슨 말인지 잘 모르겠어요.

c. 무슨 말인지 잘 들었어요.   d. 무슨 말인지 못 들었어요.

Section III - Complete the Dialogue

Choose the most appropriate expression from the box and write it in the blank.
Each answer is used only once.

> • 무슨 말이에요? 카메라도 없잖아요.
>
> • 그만둘 거라고요? 갑자기 무슨 소리예요?
>
> • 무슨 소리예요? 제가 왜요?
>
> • 무슨 말인지 잘 모르겠어요.
>
> • 무슨 말인지 알겠어요.

12. A: ︴︴︴︴︴︴︴︴︴︴︴︴︴︴︴︴︴︴︴︴︴︴

B: 다행이네요.

13. A: 다혜 씨, 이거 다혜 씨가 다 해야 돼요.

B: ︴︴︴︴︴︴︴︴︴︴︴︴︴︴︴︴︴︴︴

14. A: ︴︴︴︴︴︴︴︴︴︴︴︴︴︴︴︴︴︴︴︴

B: 다시 설명할게요. 잘 들어 보세요.

15. A: ︴︴︴︴︴︴︴︴︴︴︴︴︴︴︴︴︴︴︴

B: 갑자기 아니에요. 사실 오래전부터 생각하고 있었어요.

16. A: 카메라를 팔 거예요.

B: ︴︴︴︴︴︴︴︴︴︴︴︴︴︴︴︴︴︴︴

Section IV - Dictation

Listen to the sentences and fill in the blanks with the missing word or phrase.
The sentences will be played twice.

17. ︴︴︴︴︴︴︴︴︴︴︴︴︴︴︴︴︴︴︴︴︴ ?

18. ︴︴︴︴︴︴︴︴︴︴︴︴︴︴︴︴︴︴︴︴ .

Section V - Listening Comprehension

Listen to the dialogue and answer the following questions. The dialogue will be played twice.

19. If this conversation happened in December, in what month is Jooyeon's birthday?

a. 11월   b. 12월   c. 1월   d. 알 수 없다.

20. Choose what you can learn from the dialogue.

a. Seokjin has not bought a birthday present for Jooyeon.

b. The woman has not bought a birthday present for Jooyeon.

c. Seokjin has not bought a birthday present for Kyeong-eun.

d. The woman has not bought a birthday present for Kyeong-eun.

Section VI - Speaking Practice

A native speaker will read the dialogue from Section V line by line. Listen and repeat each sentence one by one. You can check out the dialogue in the Answer Key at the back of the book.

Lesson 13.
Word Builder #10

과(過)

Section I - Vocabulary

Choose a Korean word from the box and write it next to its correct English definition.

| 과신 | 과식 | 통과 | 과민 | 과민 반응 | 과정 |
| 과속 | 과로 | 과소비 | 과거 | 과대 | 간과 |

1. the past =

2. pass, passing through, passing (a test) =

3. overreaction =

4. too big, oversized =

5. eating too much, overeating =

6. overspending =

7. overconfidence =

8. failure to notice, passing over =

9. speeding =

10. working too much, too much labor =

11. being hypersensitive =

12. process =

Section II - Comprehension

Choose the Korean sentence or phrase that best fits the meaning of the English sentence.

13. I spent too much money.

    a. 과대(過大)했어요.   *b.* 과신(過信)했어요.

    c. 과소비(過消費)했어요.   *d.* 간과(看過)했어요.

14. I think I overlooked it.

    a. 제가 간과(看過)한 것 같아요.

    b. 제가 통과(通過)한 것 같아요.

    c. 제가 과식(過食)한 것 같아요.

    d. 제가 과속(過速)한 것 같아요.

15. I drove too fast.

    a. 과로(過勞)했어요.   *b.* 과신(過信)했어요.

    c. 과대(過大)했어요.   *d.* 과속(過速)했어요.

16. nervous person

    a. 신경이 과식(過食)한 사람   *b.* 신경이 통과(通過)한 사람

    c. 신경이 과민(過敏)한 사람   *d.* 신경이 과로(過勞)한 사람

17. It's the effort that counts, not the result.

    a. 결과보다 과로(過勞)가 중요해요.   * 결과 = result

    b. 결과보다 과정(過程)이 중요해요.

    c. 결과보다 통과(通過)가 중요해요.

    d. 결과보다 과거(過去)가 중요해요.

Section III - Complete the Dialogue

Complete each dialogue by using a word from the box.

과거	과민	과식	과속	통과	과대

18. A: 어, 여기 학교 앞이에요. _____ 하면 안 돼요.

    B: 그러네요! 알려 줘서 고마워요.　　　　　　　* 알려 주다 = to let someone know

19. A: 여보세요? 잘 안 들려요.

    B: 지금 터널 안이에요. 터널을 _____ 하고 다시 전화할게요.

20. A: 오늘은 _____ 시제를 배울 거예요.

    B: _____ 시제는 어제 배웠어요. 오늘은 미래 시제를 공부해야 돼요.

21. A: 경화 씨, 어제 본 영화 재미있었어요?

    B: 아니요. 그 영화는 너무 _____ 평가된 것 같아요.

22. A: 승완 씨, 배부르지 않아요?

    B: 배부른데, 너무 맛있어서 계속 들어가네요.

    A: _____ 은 몸에 안 좋아요. 그만 먹어요.

Section IV - Dictation

Listen to the sentences and fill in the blanks with the missing word or phrase.
The sentences will be played twice.

23. _____ .

24. _____ .

Section V – Listening Comprehension

Listen to the dialogue and answer the following questions. The dialogue will be played twice.

* 봉투 = bag
* 이만큼 = this much

25. What are they talking about?

    a. The price of the snacks

    b. The packaging of the snacks

    c. The number of snacks

    d. The taste of the snacks

26. Choose the drawing that best fits the dialogue.

a.

b.

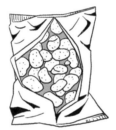

c.

d.

Section VI – Speaking Practice

A native speaker will read the dialogue from Section V line by line. Listen and repeat one by one. You can check out the dialogue in the Answer Key at the back of the book.

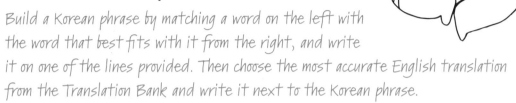

Lesson 14. 동사 + -(으)ㄹ 겸
So one can also + verb

Section I - Vocabulary

Build a Korean phrase by matching a word on the left with
the word that best fits with it from the right, and write
it on one of the lines provided. Then choose the most accurate English translation
from the Translation Bank and write it next to the Korean phrase.

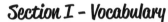

Translation Bank

to come outside	to go to Namsan	to take a walk
to look for some clothes	to take some photos	to buy a present
to get some fresh air	to read a novel	

---

1. 바람(을)   가다

2. 밖(에)   찍다

3. 소설(을)   좀 쐬다

4. 선물(을)   보다

5. 산책(을)   읽다

6. 옷(을)   사다

7. 사진(을)   하다

8. 남산(에)   나오다

1. _____

2. _____

3. _____

4. _____

5. _____

6. _____

7. _____

8. _____

Section II - Writing Practice

Write the sentences using the following structure and the words given in the parentheses. An example has been provided.

Structure:

-도 -(으)ㄹ 겸 -(으)ㄹ 거예요. = I am going to [verb] to [verb] as well.

Example: (친구를 만나다, 바다를 보다, 제주도에 가다)

친구도 만날 겸, 바다도 볼 겸, 제주도에 갈 거예요.

= I'm going to go to Jeju Island to meet my friend and also to see the sea.

9. (한국어 공부를 하다, 한국어로 된 소설을 읽다)

   ~~~~~~.

   = I'm going to read a novel written in Korean to study Korean as well.

10. (회의를 하다, 커피를 마시다, 카페에 가다)

   ~~~~~~.

   = I'm going to go to a cafe to have a meeting and also to drink some coffee.

11. (책을 읽다, 공부를 하다, 도서관에 가다)

   ~~~~~~.

   = I'm going to go to the library to read books and also to study.

12. (운동을 하다, 좀 걷다)

   ~~~~~~.

   = I am going to walk a little to do some exercise as well.

Structure:

-도 -(으)ㄹ 겸 -았/었/였어요. = I did [something] to [verb] as well.

Example: (바람 좀 쐬다, 친구 생일 선물을 사다, 밖에 나오다)

바람도 좀 쐴 겸, 친구 생일 선물도 살 겸, 밖에 나왔어요.

= I came outside to get some fresh air and also to buy a present for
  my friend's birthday.

13. (맛있는 음식을 먹다, 바다를 보다, 부산에 가다)

~~~~~~ .

= I went to Busan to eat good food and also to see the sea.

14. (선생님을 만나다, 학교에 가다)

~~~~~~ .

= I went to school to see my teacher as well.

15. (옷을 보다, 점심을 먹다, 백화점에 오다)

~~~~~~ .

= I came to the department store to look for some clothes and also to have lunch.

16. (같이 영화를 보다, 이야기를 나누다, 현우 씨를 만나다)

~~~~~~ .

= I met Hyunwoo to watch a movie together and also to talk.

Section III - Complete the Dialogue

Complete each dialogue below using one of the sentences from Section II.

17. A: 도서관에서 공부할 거예요?

   B: 네. ~~~~~~ .

18. A: 어제 학교 갔어요?

   B: 네. ~~~~~~ .

19. A: 예지 씨, 또 백화점이에요?

B: 네. 〰〰〰〰〰〰〰〰〰〰〰〰〰〰〰〰〰〰〰〰〰〰〰.

20. A: 어제 현우 씨 만났어요?

B: 〰〰〰〰〰〰〰〰〰〰〰〰〰〰〰〰〰〰〰〰〰〰〰.

21. A: 어떤 책 읽을 거예요?

B: 〰〰〰〰〰〰〰〰〰〰〰〰〰〰〰〰〰〰〰〰〰〰〰.

22. A: 휴가 때 어디 갔어요?

B: 〰〰〰〰〰〰〰〰〰〰〰〰〰〰〰〰〰〰〰〰〰〰〰.

Section IV - Dictation

Listen to the sentences and fill in the blanks with the missing word or phrase. The sentences will be played twice.

23. 주연 씨는 〰〰〰〰〰〰〰〰〰〰〰〰〰〰〰〰〰〰 예요.

24. A: 어제 남산에 갔어요?

B: 네. 〰〰〰〰〰〰〰〰〰〰〰〰〰〰〰〰〰〰〰.

Section V - Listening Comprehension

Listen to the dialogue and answer the following questions. The dialogue will be played twice.

* 계란 = egg
* 식빵 = sliced bread
* 쓰레기 = trash

25. Choose the correct statement according to the dialogue.

    a. The son is going to take out the trash.

    b. The mom is going to take out the trash.

    c. The son is going to go grocery shopping tomorrow.

    d. The mom is going to go grocery shopping tomorrow.

26. What is another purpose of the son going to the supermarket?

    a. 바람도 쐴 겸

    b. 친구 생일 선물도 살 겸

    c. 운동도 할 겸

    d. 운전 연습도 할 겸

Section VI - Speaking Practice

A native speaker will read the dialogue from Section V line by line.
Listen and repeat each sentence one by one. You can check out the
dialogue in the Answer Key at the back of the book.

Lesson 15.   -(이)라는 것은
The thing that is called,
What they call...

Section I - Vocabulary

Choose a Korean word from the box and write it next to its corresponding English definition.

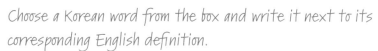

| 진정한 친구 | 꿈 | 삶 | 사람의 마음 |
| 우정 | 자유 | 행복 | 부자 |

1. freedom =

2. rich man =

3. friendship =

4. a person's mind/heart =

5. life =

6. dream =

7. true friend =

8. happiness =

Section II - Comprehension

Translate each phrase into Korean using -(이)라는 것은, and then shorten it using -(이)란. Use the words and phrases from Section I - Vocabulary. The first one has been done for you.

9. I think happiness is... = 행복이라는 것은 ➔ 행복이란

10. A rich man is... = _____ ➔ _____

11. What they call "friendship" is... = _____ ➔ _____

12. I think a person's mind/heart is... = _____ ➔ _____

13. Life is... = _____ ➔ _____

14. A dream is... = _____ ➔ _____

15. I think a true friend is... = _____ ➔ _____

Section III - Fill in the Blank

Fill in the blanks using -(이)란 and the phrases from Section II - Comprehension. Each expression is used only once. An example has been provided.

Ex)

제가 생각하는 행복이란 좋아하는 사람들과 같이 있는 거예요.

(= I think happiness is being with people I like.)

16. _____ 어려울 때 도와주는 친구예요.

17. _____ 쉽게 이룰 수 없는 거예요.   * 이루다 = to achieve

18. _____ 사랑의 다른 이름이에요.

19. _____ 돈이 많은 사람이라는 뜻이에요.

20. A: _____ 알 수 없는 거예요.

    B: 아니에요. 저는 다혜 씨 마음을 다 알 수 있어요.

21. A: 너무 아픈데 출근해야 돼요.

    B: _____ 원래 그런 거예요. 쉽지 않아요.

    * 원래 = originally, actually

Section IV - Dictation

Listen to the sentences and fill in the blanks with the missing word or phrase. The sentences will be played twice.

22. _____, 아무거나 마음대로 하는 것이 아니에요.

23. _____.

Section V - Listening Comprehension

Listen to the dialogue and answer the following questions. The dialogue will be played twice.

* 피츠버그 파이어리츠 = Pittsburgh Pirates, an American professional baseball team
* 성적 = score, * 꾸준히 = constantly, * 응원하다 = to cheer

24. Is Kyung-hwa a fan of the Pittsburgh Pirates?

    a. 알 수 없어요.

    b. 네, 팬이에요.

    c. 아니요, 팬이 아니에요.

25. Who is on the same page as Kyung-hwa about what true fans are? Write
    the person's name.

> 윤아: 응원은 중요하지 않아요.
>
> 예지: 다음 경기에서 이기면 응원할 거예요.
>
> 다혜: 팀 성적이 안 좋아도 계속 응원할 거예요!
>
> 보람: 저는 성적을 확인하지 않아요.

    Answer: _____

Section VI - Speaking Practice

A native speaker will read the dialogue from Section V line by line.
Listen and repeat each sentence one by one. You can check out the
dialogue in the Answer Key at the back of the book.

Lesson 16.
Various Usages of the Suffix -겠-

Section I - Vocabulary

Match each Korean word to its common English translation.

1. 다녀오다   a. by oneself, on one's own

2. 들어가다   b. to feel sleepy

3. 힘들다   c. to die

4. 상자   d. to go in, to fit in

5. 죽다   e. box

6. 뵙다   f. to go to a place and come back

7. 졸리다   g. to be hard, to be tough

8. 혼자   h. to humbly see/meet

9. 아프다   i. to be sick, to hurt

Section II - Comprehension

10. Select the answer that is a more formal version of, "어디로 가실래요?"

   a. 어디로 갈래요?

   b. 어디로 가요?

   c. 어디로 갔습니까?

   d. 어디로 가시겠어요?

11. What do Koreans say before eating a meal?

   a. 잘 먹었습니다.

   b. 잘 먹겠습니다.

   c. 정말 배부르겠습니다.

   d. 정말 배불렀습니다.

12. Choose the sentence that does NOT have the meaning of, "I will not tell you."

   a. 말 안 할 거예요.

   b. 말하지 않겠습니다.

   c. 말하지 않았을 거예요.

   d. 말하지 않을 거예요.

13. Change the underlined section using -시겠어요 to make the sentence sound much more formal.

   뭐 좀 먹을래요? ↣ 뭐 좀 ____________?

14. Write the answer that can fill in both of the blanks.

   • 배고파 ____________. = I'm so hungry; I'm going to die.

• 졸려 <u>＿＿＿＿＿＿＿＿＿＿＿</u>. = I'm so tired; I'm going to die.

Section III - Complete the Dialogue

Choose the most appropriate word or phrase from the box and write it in the blank using -겠어요.

아프다	들어가다	늦다	좋다	잘 모르다	전화해 주다

15. A: 아야!

    B: <u>＿＿＿＿＿＿＿＿＿＿＿＿＿＿＿＿＿＿＿</u>.

16. A: 어떤 가방을 살까요?

    B: 이게 <u>＿＿＿＿＿＿＿＿＿＿＿＿＿＿＿＿＿＿</u>.

17. A: 지금 몇 시예요?

    B: 9시 50분이에요. 빨리 해요. <u>＿＿＿＿＿＿＿＿＿＿＿＿＿＿</u>.

18. A: 이 상자 진짜 크죠?

    B: 네. 저도 <u>＿＿＿＿＿＿＿＿＿＿＿＿＿＿＿＿＿</u>.

19. A: 이 사람 알아요?

    B: <u>＿＿＿＿＿＿＿＿＿＿＿＿＿＿＿＿＿＿＿</u>.

20. A: 지금 통화할 수 있어요?

    B: 죄송합니다. 지금 회의 중인데, 한 시간 후에 다시 <u>＿＿＿＿＿＿＿＿</u>?

Section IV – Dictation

Listen to the sentences and fill in the blanks with the missing word or phrase. The sentences will be played twice.

21. 제가 ＿＿＿＿＿＿＿＿＿＿＿＿＿＿＿＿＿＿＿＿ .

22. ＿＿＿＿＿＿＿＿＿＿＿＿＿＿＿＿＿＿＿＿＿＿ ?

Section V – Listening Comprehension

Listen to the dialogue and answer the following questions. The dialogue will be played twice.

* 야식 = late-night snack

23. Which statement is correct according to the dialogue?

    a. The man has decided to have a late-night snack.

    b. The man has decided to eat anything he wants after 6 o'clock.

    c. The man has decided not to eat anything after 6 o'clock.

    d. The man has decided not to eat anything for a while.

24. What does the woman think about the man's resolution?

    a. The woman thinks that the man will break his resolution.

    b. The woman thinks that the man will be able to stick to his resolution.

    c. The woman does not understand the man's resolution.

    d. The woman thinks that sticking to the resolution will be hard.

Section VI – Speaking Practice

A native speaker will read the dialogue from Section V line by line. Listen and repeat each sentence one by one. You can check out the dialogue in the Answer Key at the back of the book.

Lesson 17.
Because, Since, Let me tell you...

-거든(요)

Section I - Vocabulary

Choose a Korean word from the box and write it next to its correct English definition.

좀	방금	필요	이미	계속
끝내다	때문에	빌려주다	아까	

1. to lend =

2. continuously, constantly =

3. a little =

4. earlier, a little while ago =

5. to finish =

6. just (now) =

7. need, necessity =

8. already =

Section II - Conjugation Practice

Fill in the blanks by conjugating the words in the box using -거든요. Each word is used only once.

| 되다 | 끝내다 | 늦다 | 만나다 | 가다 | 바쁘다 |

9. 지난주에 제주도에 _____. 그런데 계속 비가 왔어요.

= I went to Jeju Island last week. But it kept raining.

10. 아까 현우 씨 _____. 그런데 이상한 말을 했어요.

= I met Hyunwoo earlier. But he said something strange.

11. 나중에 이야기해도 돼요? 제가 지금 좀 _____.

= Can we talk later? I'm a little busy now.

12. 이미 _____!

= It's already too late!

13. _____!

= It's over. / I don't need that.

14. 내일은 안 바빠요. 오늘 일을 다 _____.

= I'm not busy tomorrow. (Because) I finished all my work today.

Section III - Reading Comprehension

Using -거든(요), complete the dialogue below about the Hanguk University Graduation Concert.

한국대학교 2020 졸업 공연

- 언제? 2020.12.11. (금)~2020.12.12. (토)

- 어디서? 한국대학교 대강당

- 얼마? 1,000원 (팸플릿 사면 무료)

- 무엇을? 2020 졸업 공연 (1부: 춤, 2부: 노래)

	12/11	12/12
15:00	김예지, 선경화	김희주, 석다혜
19:00	김희주, 석다혜	김예지, 선경화

* Vocabulary

공연 = performance, concert

팸플릿 = pamphlet

부 = part, section

대강당 = main hall, auditorium

무료 = free of charge

현우: 나 어젯밤에 한국대학교 졸업 공연 보고 왔어.

경은: 정말? 어땠어?

현우: 춤도 추고 노래도 15. _____. 진짜 재밌었어.

경은: 오! 진짜 재밌었겠다. 얼마였어?

현우: 무료였어. 나는 팸플릿을 ¹⁶.~~~~~~~~~~~~~~~~~~~~~~~.

경은: 팸플릿 안 사면 얼마야?

현우: 팸플릿 안 사면 천 원이야. 갈 거면 천 원 가져가.

경은: 알겠어. 참, 경화도 봤어?

현우: 아니. 경화는 어제 3시에 공연을 ¹⁷.~~~~~~~~~~~~~~~~~~.

경은: 아하! 내일도 경화 3시에 공연해?

현우: 내일이 13일이지? 내일은 경화 공연 못 봐.

　　　오늘이 마지막 ¹⁸.~~~~~~~~~~~~~~~.

경은: 정말?

현우: 응. 오늘 7시가 마지막 공연이야.

경은: 그럼 혹시 천 원만 빌려줄 수 있어? 내가 지금 돈이 ¹⁹.~~~~~~~~~~~~.

Section IV - Dictation

Listen to the sentences and fill in the blanks with the missing word or phrase. The sentences will be played twice.

20. ~~~~~~!

21. A: 현우 씨, 이게 무슨 일이에요?

　　B: 저도 모르겠네요. 사실 저도 ~~~~~~~~~~~~~~~~~~~~~~.

Section V - Listening Comprehension

22. Listen to the dialogue and choose which statements are correct and which are incorrect. The dialogue will be played twice.

*표정 = look, face
*몸살감기 = a bad cold
*퇴근하다 = to leave work

a. Before this conversation, the man knew why Jooyeon did not look too good today.

b. Before this conversation, the woman knew why Jooyeon did not look too good today.

c. The man is worried that Jooyeon might catch a bad cold.

d. The woman is worried that Jooyeon is going to catch a bad cold.

- Correct statements: _____
- Incorrect statements: _____

Section VI - Speaking Practice

A native speaker will read the dialogue from Section V line by line. Listen and repeat each sentence one by one. You can check out the dialogue in the Answer Key at the back of the book.

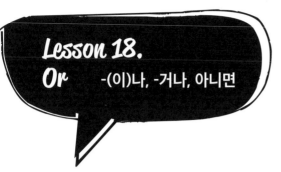

Lesson 18.
Or -(이)나, -거나, 아니면

Section I - Vocabulary

Build a Korean phrase by matching a word on the left with the word that best fits with it from the right, and write it on one of the lines provided. Choose the most accurate English translation from the Translation Bank and write it next to the Korean phrase. All words and phrases are used in the following sections as well, so be sure to commit them to memory!

Translation Bank

to send a text message   to eat gimbap   to meet a friend

to eat cake   to ride a bicycle   to buy a hat

to dance   to take the subway

---

1. 케이크를

2. 자전거를

3. 문자를

4. 지하철을

5. 춤을

6. 모자를

7. 김밥을

8. 친구를

만나다

추다

타다

사다

보내다

타다

먹다

1.

_____

2.

_____

3.

_____

4.

_____

5.

_____

6.

_____

7.

_____

8.

_____

Section II - Comprehension

Complete the dialogues using -(이)나 or -거나 based on each of the drawings.

9.

A: 뭐 먹을 거예요?

B: ＿＿＿＿＿＿＿＿＿＿＿＿＿ 를
먹을 거예요.

10.

A: 어떻게 연락할 거예요?

B: 〰〰〰〰〰〰〰〰〰〰〰〰〰〰〰〰〰〰〰

문자를 보낼 거예요.

11.

A: 회사에 어떻게 가요?

B: 〰〰〰〰〰〰〰〰〰〰〰〰〰〰〰〰〰을

타고 가요.

12.

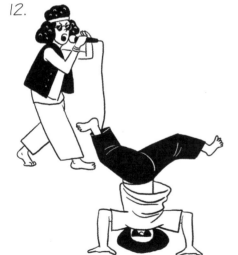

A: 동근 씨, 장기 자랑에서 뭐 할 거예요?

* 장기 자랑 = talent show

B: 〰〰〰〰〰〰〰〰〰〰〰〰〰〰〰〰〰

출 거예요.

13.

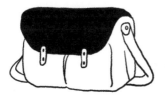

A: 뭐 살 거예요?

B: ＿＿＿＿＿＿＿＿＿＿＿＿＿＿＿＿＿＿

를 살 거예요.

14.

A: 경화 씨, 배고프면 ＿＿＿＿＿＿＿＿＿ 를

좀 마셔요.

B: 고마워요. 커피를 좀 마실게요.

15.

A: 주말에 뭐 할 거예요?

B: ＿＿＿＿＿＿＿＿＿＿＿＿＿ 읽을 거예요.

Section III - Reading Comprehension

Read the following text messages between Dahye and Yeji and answer the questions.

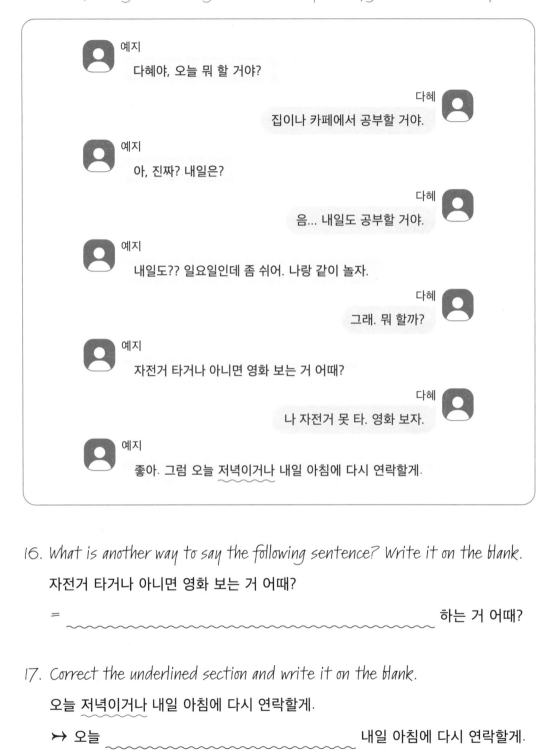

예지
다혜야, 오늘 뭐 할 거야?

다혜
집이나 카페에서 공부할 거야.

예지
아, 진짜? 내일은?

다혜
음... 내일도 공부할 거야.

예지
내일도?? 일요일인데 좀 쉬어. 나랑 같이 놀자.

다혜
그래. 뭐 할까?

예지
자전거 타거나 아니면 영화 보는 거 어때?

다혜
나 자전거 못 타. 영화 보자.

예지
좋아. 그럼 오늘 저녁이거나 내일 아침에 다시 연락할게.

16. What is another way to say the following sentence? Write it on the blank.

자전거 타거나 아니면 영화 보는 거 어때?

= _____ 하는 거 어때?

17. Correct the underlined section and write it on the blank.

오늘 저녁이거나 내일 아침에 다시 연락할게.

→ 오늘 _____ 내일 아침에 다시 연락할게.

18. Write the three-letter word that can be used in all of the following sentences.

> - 다혜야, 내일 집에서 공부할 거야? ～～～～ 카페에서 공부할 거야?
> - 다혜야, 내일 자전거 탈 거야? ～～～～ 영화 볼 거야?
> - 예지야, 오늘 저녁에 연락할 거야? ～～～～ 내일 아침에 연락할 거야?

Answer: ～～～～～～

19. Choose the correct statement according to the text messages above.

a. Dahye is not going to study at home.

b. Dahye is not going to study at a cafe.

c. Dahye and Yeji are not going to watch a movie today.

d. Yeji is not going to contact Dahye tomorrow morning.

Section IV - Dictation

Listen to the sentences and fill in the blanks with the missing word or phrase. The sentences will be played twice.

20. ～～～～～～～～～～～ 집에 갈 거예요.

21. ～～～～～～～～～～～～～～～～～～ .

Section V - Listening Comprehension

Listen to the dialogue and answer the following questions. The dialogue will be played twice.

* 주로 = usually
* 밀리다 = to be left undone

22. Choose what Hyunwoo did NOT say he does on the weekend.

a.

b.

c.

d.

23. Choose the correct statement according to the dialogue.

    a. Hyunwoo usually leaves his homework undone on the weekend.

    b. Hyunwoo usually reads books on the weekend.

    c. Hyunwoo sometimes meets up with his friends on the weekend.

    d. Hyunwoo rides his bicycle every weekend.

Section VI - Speaking Practice

A native speaker will read the dialogue from Section V line by line.
Listen and repeat each sentence one by one. You can check out the
dialogue in the Answer Key at the back of the book.

Section I - Vocabulary

Translate each word into English or your preferred language. Then, choose its antonym from the box and write it down. The first one has been done for you. (Translations in the Answer Key are given in English.)

쉽다	좁다	적다	같다	가깝다
시끄럽다	더럽다	작다	길다	덥다

1. 깨끗하다 (= *to be clean*) ↔ 더럽다

2. 멀다 (=) ↔

3. 춥다 (=) ↔

4. 조용하다 (=) ↔

5. 짧다 (=) ↔

6. 어렵다 (=) ↔

7. 많다 (=) ↔

8. 다르다 (=) ↔

9. 크다 (=) ↔

10. 넓다 (=) ↔

Section II - Comprehension

Fill in the blanks using -아/어/여졌어요 with the words from Section I - Vocabulary.

11. 날씨가 〜〜〜〜〜〜〜〜〜〜〜〜〜〜〜〜〜〜〜〜〜〜〜〜〜〜〜〜〜〜〜〜 .

12. 프랑스어 공부가 〜〜〜〜〜〜〜〜〜〜〜〜〜〜〜〜〜〜〜〜〜〜〜〜〜〜 .

13. 방이 〜〜〜〜〜〜〜〜〜〜〜〜〜〜〜〜〜〜〜〜〜〜〜〜〜〜〜〜〜〜〜〜〜〜 .

14. 줄이 〰〰〰〰〰〰〰〰〰〰〰〰〰〰〰〰〰〰〰〰〰〰〰〰.

15. 교실이 〰〰〰〰〰〰〰〰〰〰〰〰〰〰〰〰〰〰〰〰〰.

16. 키가 〰〰〰〰〰〰〰〰〰〰〰〰〰〰〰〰〰〰〰〰〰〰〰.

Section III - Complete the Dialogue

Complete each dialogue by using a word in the box with -아/어/여지다. Each word is used only once.

조용하다   좋다   따뜻하다   가깝다   작다

17. A: 회사가 멀어요?

    B: 옛날에는 멀었어요. 지금은 이사해서 ~~~~~~~~~~~~~~~~~~~~~~.

18. A: 살이 쪄서 옷이 ~~~~~~~~~~~~~~~~~~~~~.

    *살이 찌다 = *to gain weight*

    B: 저랑 같이 운동할래요?

19. A: 다혜 씨, 아직도 추워요?

    B: 아니요. 이제 좀 ~~~~~~~~~~~~~~~~~~~~~. 감사해요.

20. A: 캐시 씨, 한국어 발음이 정말 ~~~~~~~~~~~~~~~~~~~~~.

    B: 감사합니다. 매일매일 연습했어요.

21. A: 어, 갑자기 ~~~~~~~~~~~~~~~~~~~~~.

    B: 아이들이 자나 봐요.

Section IV - Dictation

Listen to the sentences and fill in the blanks with the missing word or phrase. The sentences will be played twice.

22. 한국으로 여행 오는 사람들이 ～～～～～～～～～～～～～～～ .

23. ～～～～～～～～～～～～～～～～～～～ .

Section V - Listening Comprehension

Listen to the dialogue and answer the following questions. The dialogue will be played twice.

*예전 = before, * 직원 = employee

24. What has changed about the office according to the dialogue? More than one answer may be possible.

    a. the number of employees   b. cafeteria   c. location   d. size

25. What is the man likely to say right after this dialogue?

    a. 회사가 커졌어요?   b. 너무 좁아진 것 같아요.

    c. 정말 축하해요.   d. 정말 많아졌네요.

Section VI - Speaking Practice

A native speaker will read the dialogue from Section V line by line. Listen and repeat each sentence one by one. You can check out the dialogue in the Answer Key at the back of the book.

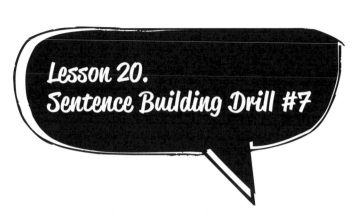

Lesson 20.
Sentence Building Drill #7

Section I - Vocabulary

Complete the dialogue by using words from the box below. Remember to conjugate the words when necessary.

부탁하다	백화점	문자	알아보다	나가다	가격

경화: 우와, 이 가방 샀어요?

다혜: 네. 지난주에 1. _____ 으로 쇼핑 가서 샀어요.

경화: 얼마였어요?

다혜: 200,000원이요.

경화: 우와, 진짜 비싸네요! 제가 인터넷에서 본 2. _____ 은 150,000원이었어요.

다혜: 정말요?

경화: 네. 다음에는 인터넷으로 먼저 3. ~~~~~~~~~~~~~~~고 사세요.

다혜: 저 그런 거 잘 못하는데, 혹시 경화 씨한테 4. ~~~~~~~~~~~~~~~도 돼요?

경화: 네. 그럼 다음에 뭐 살 때 저한테 5. ~~~~~~~~~~~~~~~보내세요.

다혜: 네. 고마워요. 사실 내일도 6. ~~~~~~~~~~~~~~~서 쇼핑하려고 했는데…

　　　혹시 시간 되면 저랑 같이 쇼핑 갈래요?

Section II - Comprehension

Complete the sentences by conjugating the word in the parentheses using either "-(으)ㄹ 겸", "-(으)거나 아니면", or "-(으)ㄹ 거라고요", depending on which fits best. Then translate each sentence into English.

-(으)ㄹ 겸　　-(으)거나 아니면　　-(으)ㄹ 거라고요

7. 핸드폰 가격도 ~~~~~~~~~~~~~~~~~~, 홍대에 갔어요. (알아보다)

　　=

8. 여기에서 ~~~~~~~~~~~~~~~~나가서 커피 마시고 있을게요. (기다리다)

　　=

9. 그러니까 혼자 ~~~~~~~~~~~~~~~? (오다)

　　=

10. 공부도 ~~~~~~~~~~~~~~, 친구도 ~~~~~~~~~~~~~~,
　　도서관에 갈 수도 있어요. (하다, 만나다)

　　=

11. 그러니까 언제 _____? (하다)

    =

12. 석진 씨한테 _____ 그냥 제가 해 볼게요. (부탁하다)

    =

Section III - Complete the Dialogue

Complete each dialogue by taking a sentence fragment from column A and matching it with the fragment that best fits with it from column B. Each fragment is used only once.

A	B
• 두루 씨한테 물어보거나	• 카페에서 해요.
• 그러니까 다음 주에	• 지난달이었다고요?
• 오늘 저녁에 전화하거나	• 프랑스에 갈 거라고요?
• 예지 씨 생일 선물도 살 겸	• 아니면 인터넷으로 알아볼게요.
• 커피도 마실 겸	• 백화점에 갈 거예요.
• 그러니까 승완 씨 생일이	• 아니면 문자 보낼게요.

13. A: 어디에서 회의할까요?

    B: _____

14. A: 미안해요. 저도 잘 모르겠어요.

    B: 아니에요. 괜찮아요. _____

15. A: ~~~~~~

  B: 네. 늦게 말해서 미안해요. 가서 연락할게요.

16. A: 오후에 어디 갈 거예요?

  B: ~~~~~~

17. A: ~~~~~~

  B: 네. 승완 씨 생일은 2월 25일이었어요.

18. A: ~~~~~~

  B: 네. 기다릴게요. 저녁에 꼭 연락 주세요.

Section IV - Dictation

Listen to the sentences and fill in the blanks with the missing word or phrase. The sentences will be played twice.

19. ~~~~~~~~~~~~~~~~~~~~ 다시 ~~~~~~~~~~~~~~~~~~~~ 있어요.

20. 그러니까 ~~~~~~ ?

Section V - Listening Comprehension

Listen to the dialogue and answer the following questions. The dialogue will be played twice.

* 유튜브 = YouTube, an online video-sharing platform
* 팟캐스트 = podcast, an online audio-broadcasting platform

21. Why did the man named Mark say he often watches Korean dramas? Fill in the boxes in Korean using -도 -(으)ㄹ 겸.

마크: "⬚⬚⬚ ⬚⬚⬚ ⬚⬚

한국 드라마를 자주 봐요."

22. How did the woman named Cassie say she studies Korean? Fill in the boxes in Korean using -거나 아니면.

캐시: "⬚⬚⬚ ⬚⬚ ⬚⬚⬚ ⬚⬚

팟캐스트 많이 들어요."

Section VI - Speaking Practice

A native speaker will read the dialogue from Section V line by line. Listen and repeat each sentence one by one. You can check out the dialogue in the Answer Key at the back of the book.

Lesson 21.
Passive Voice (Part 1)
-이/히/리/기-, -아/어/여지다

Section I - Vocabulary

Change each word to its passive form by adding the suffix -이/히/리/기- or by conjugating it using -아/어/여지다. Choose the most accurate English translation from the Translation Bank and write it next to the Korean word.

─── **Translation Bank** ───

to get cut	to be put down	to be put into	to be eaten	to get closed
to be piled up	to be washed	to be chased	to be sent	to be given
to get caught	to be pushed	to come untied	to be hugged	

1. 쌓다 ↦

2. 풀다 ↦

3. 자르다 ↦

4. 먹다 ↦

5. 쫓다 ↦

6. 잡다 ↦

7. 안다 ↦

8. 닫다 ↦

9. 보내다 ↦

10. 놓다 ↦

Section II - Fill in the Blank

Complete the description of the drawing by conjugating the passive words from Section I - Vocabulary.

Ex) 도둑이 잡혔어요.　*도둑 = thief
(= The thief has been caught.)

11. 도둑이 경찰한테 ＿＿＿＿＿＿＿＿＿.

*경찰 = police

12. 신발 끈이 ＿＿＿＿＿＿＿.

*끈 = string

13. 갑자기 문이 ＿＿＿＿＿＿＿.

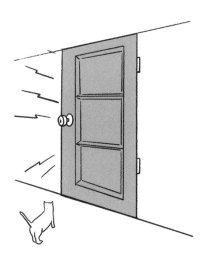

14. 밖에 눈이 많이 _____.

15. 실수로 문자가 _____.

* 실수로 = *by mistake*

16. 코끼리가 뱀한테 _____.

* 코끼리 = *elephant*, 뱀 = *snake*

17. 강아지가 저한테 _____ 잠들었어요.

Section III - Comprehension

Circle the correct phrase. If both answers are possible, underline both phrases. Then translate the sentences into your preferred language. (Translations in the Answer Key are given in English.)

18. 저한테도 기회가 (주었어요/주어졌어요.)

* 기회 = *opportunity, chance*

=

19. 모자, 쇼핑백에 (담아/담겨) 드릴까요?　　　　　* 쇼핑백 = shopping bag

＝

20. 하늘을 나는 방법이 (연구하고/연구되고) 있어요.

＝

21. 저 어제 지하철에서 사람들한테 (밀어서/밀려서) 넘어졌어요.

＝　　　　　　　　　　　　　　　　　　* 넘어지다 = to fall down

22. Talk To Me In Korean 웹사이트를 (이용하는/이용되는) 사람들이 많아지고 있
어요.

＝

Section IV - Dictation

Listen to the sentences and fill in the blanks with the missing word or phrase.
The sentences will be played twice.

23. 열쇠 ＿＿＿＿＿＿＿＿ 상자 못 봤어요?

24. ' ＿＿＿＿＿＿＿＿ '가 아니고 ' ＿＿＿＿＿＿＿＿ '예요.

Section V - Listening Comprehension

25. Listen to the dialogue and choose the answer that best describes the dialogue. The dialogue will be played twice.

* 운동화 = sneakers

a.

b.

c.

d.

Section VI - Speaking Practice

A native speaker will read the dialogue from Section V line by line. Listen and repeat each sentence one by one. You can check out the dialogue in the Answer Key at the back of the book.

Lesson 22.
Word Builder #11

무(無)

Section I - Vocabulary

Match the words in the Word Bank with their correct English definition.

Word Bank

무적   무죄   무공해   무조건   무료   무시   무책임

무능력   무인   무명   무관심   무사고   무한

1. unmanned, uninhabited =

2. not popular, unknown =

3. pollution-free, clean =

4. to overlook, to neglect, to disregard =

5. unconditionally =

6. free of charge =

7. irresponsibility =

8. infinite, limitless =

9. innocent, not guilty =

10. no accident =

11. unbeatable, invincible =

12. incapability, incompetence =

13. indifference, showing no interest =

Section II - Comprehension

Select the sentence or phrase that best represents the meaning of the English translation.

14. I'm incapable.

    a. 무관심(無關心)해요.   *b.* 무능력(無能力)해요.

    c. 무책임(無責任)해요.   *d.* 무한(無限)해요.

15. Just ignore it.

    a. 그냥 무시(無視)해요.   *b.* 그냥 무공해(無公害)해요.

    c. 그냥 무한(無限)해요.   *d.* 그냥 무관심(無關心)해요.

16. irresponsible person

    a. 무명(無名)한 사람   *b.* 무관심(無關心)한 사람

    c. 무공해(無公害)한 사람   *d.* 무책임(無責任)한 사람

17. infinite love

    a. 무관심(無關心) 사랑   *b.* 무사고(無事故) 사랑

    c. 무한(無限) 사랑   *d.* 무명(無名) 사랑

18. I'm not a well-known singer.

    a. 저는 무사고(無事故) 가수예요.

    b. 저는 무공해(無公害) 가수예요.

    c. 저는 무적(無敵) 가수예요.

    d. 저는 무명(無名) 가수예요.

Section III - Complete the Dialogue

Complete each dialogue using a word from the box. Each word is used only once.

무공해	무인	무사고	무적	무료

19. A: 윤아 씨, 운전 잘해요?

    B: 네. 저 10년째 ＿＿＿＿＿ 운전 중이에요.   * -째 = *for*

20. A: 경화 씨, 돈 냈어요?

    B: 아니요. 이거 ＿＿＿＿＿ 예요.

21. A: 편의점에 사람이 아무도 없네요?   * 편의점 = *convenience store*

    B: 여기 ＿＿＿＿＿ 편의점이에요.

22. A: 우와, 또 이겼어요?

    B: 그럼요! 저희 팀은 ＿＿＿＿＿ 이에요.

23. A: 씻지 않고 바로 먹어도 돼요?

    B: ＿＿＿＿＿ 농산물은 바로 먹어도 괜찮아요.   * 농산물 = *farm produce*

Section IV - Dictation

Listen to the sentences and fill in the blanks with the missing word or phrase. The sentences will be played twice.

24. 주연 씨는 먹는 것에 ~~~~~~~~~~~~~~~~~~~~~~~~~~~.

25. ~~~~~~.

Section V - Listening Comprehension

Listen to the dialogue and answer the following questions. The dialogue will be played twice.

*역할 = role / *시절 = days
*촬영장 = set / *구석 = corner

26. What is the man's role in the movie they are talking about?

    a. 사람들이 잘 아는 배우

    b. 사람들이 잘 모르는 배우

    c. 친구가 없는 배우

    d. 친구가 많은 배우

27. Choose the correct statement according to the dialogue.

    a. The man has not become a famous actor yet.

    b. The man became famous immediately after his debut.

    c. The man cried a lot when he was an unknown actor.

    d. The man cried a lot while playing his role in the movie.

Section VI - Speaking Practice

A native speaker will read the dialogue from Section V line by line. Listen and repeat each sentence one by one. You can check out the dialogue in the Answer Key at the back of the book.

Lesson 23.
Passive Voice (Part 2)
-이/히/리/기-, -아/어/여지다

Section I - Vocabulary

Circle the correct translation of the Korean expression. All words will be used in the following sections as well, so be sure to check your answers and commit each word to memory before you move on to the next section!

1. 보이다   a. to be seen, to be visible   b. to be audible, to be heard

2. 들리다   a. to be seen, to be visible   b. to be audible, to be heard

3. 쓰이다   a. to be used   b. to be written

4. 닫히다   a. to open, to be unlocked   b. to be closed

5. 열리다   a. to open, to be unlocked   b. to be closed

6. 꺼지다   a. to be turned off   b. to be turned on

7. 켜지다   a. to be turned off   b. to be turned on

8. 풀리다   a. to come untied, to be solved   b. to be changed, to be replaced

9. 바뀌다   a. to come untied, to be solved   b. to be changed, to be replaced

Section II - Fill in the Blank

Complete the sentences using the passive forms of the words in the box.

끄다	듣다	쓰다	보다	하다	풀다	바꾸다

10. 배터리가 없어서 핸드폰이 _____ 어요. * 배터리 = battery

11. 잘 안 _____ 는데, 좀 크게 말씀해 주시겠어요?

12. 글씨가 작아서 잘 안 _____ 는데, 좀 크게 써 주세요.

13. 이해가 잘 안 _____ 는데, 한 번 더 설명해 주시겠어요?

14. 석진 씨, 이 문제 너무 안 _____ 는데, 좀 도와주세요.

15. 어? 여기 카페였는데 식당으로 _____ 었네요.

16. 프랑스어로 _____ 책이네요. 현우 씨, 프랑스어도 할 수 있어요?

Section III - Comprehension

Complete each sentence by conjugating 되다. Then translate the sentences into your preferred language. (Translations in the Answer Key are given in English.)

17. 김밥 _____ 요? =

18. 오늘 안에 _____ 요? =

19. 영어가 안 _____ 서 걱정이에요. =

20. 이거 안 ~~_____~~ 는데 좀 도와주세요. =

21. 케이크를 예쁘게 만들고 싶은데 예쁘게 안 ~~_____~~ 요. =

Section IV - Dictation

Listen to the sentences and fill in the blanks with the missing word or phrase.
The sentences will be played twice.

22. 불이 갑자기 ~~_____~~ .

23. 왜 그러는지 ~~_____~~ .

Section V - Listening Comprehension

24. Listen to the dialogue and choose the drawing that best describes the
    status of the woman's cell phone. The dialogue will be played twice.

a.    b.   c.    d.

Section VI - Speaking Practice

A native speaker will read the dialogue from Section V line by line.
Listen and repeat each sentence one by one. You can check out the
dialogue in the Answer Key at the back of the book.

Lesson 24.
I DID do it, but...;
I DO like it, but...

-기는 하다

Section I - Vocabulary

Fill in the chart. The first word has been done for you.

Verb	Meaning	Present Tense: Verb + -기는 Verb + -아/어/여요.	Past Tense: Verb + -기는 Verb + -았/었/였어요.	Future Tense: Verb + -기는 Verb + -(으)ㄹ 거예요.
1. 만나다	to meet	만나기는 만나요.	만나기는 만났어요.	만나기는 만날 거예요.
2. 헤어지다				
3. 준비하다				
4. 도착하다				

Adjective	Meaning	Present Tense: Verb + -기는 Verb + -아/어/여요.	Past Tense: Verb + -기는 Verb + -았/었/였어요.	Future Tense: Verb + -기는 Verb + -(으)ㄹ 거예요.
5. 좋다				
6. 짜다				
7. 춥다				
8. 맛있다				

Section II - Comprehension

Combine the two sentences by using -기는 -(으/느)ㄴ데, then translate them into your preferred language. (Answers are provided in English only.) The first one has been done for you.

9. 봤어요. 그런데 기억이 안 나요.

→ 보기는 봤는데, 기억이 안 나요. or 보기는 했는데, 기억이 안 나요.

= I DID see it, but I don't remember.

10. 갔어요. 그런데 일찍 나왔어요.

→

＝

11. 경은 씨를 만났어요. 그런데 금방 헤어졌어요.

→

＝

12. 읽었어요. 그런데 아직도 무슨 말인지 잘 모르겠어요.

→

＝

13. 짜요. 그런데 맛있어요.

→

＝

14. 멀어요. 그런데 오늘 꼭 가야 돼요.

→

＝

15. 아직 추워요. 그런데 괜찮아요.

→

＝

Section III - Complete the Dialogue

Complete the dialogues below by using the combined sentences from Section II. Each sentence is used only once.

16. A: 어제 경은 씨 만났어요?

B: _____.

17. A: 이 드라마 봤어요?

B: ~~~~~~ .

18. A: 김치찌개 맛이 어때요?

B: ~~~~~~ .

19. A: 한국은 아직도 춥죠?

B: ~~~~~~ .

20. A: 준배 씨, 이 책 읽었죠? 너무 어렵지 않았어요?

B: 네. ~~~~~~ .

21. A: 지금 지나 씨 집에 간다고요? 너무 멀지 않아요?

B: ~~~~~~ .

22. A: 다혜 씨도 어제 졸업 파티 갔어요?

B: ~~~~~~ .

Section IV - Dictation

Listen to the sentences and fill in the blanks with the missing word or phrase. The sentences will be played twice.

23. ~~~~~~~~~~~~~~~~~~~~~~~~~~~~~~~~~~~~ , 너무 비싼 것 같아요.

24. ~~~~~~ , 준비를 못 했어요.

Section V - Listening Comprehension

True/False – Listen to the dialogue and decide if each statement is true or false. Write "T" if the statement is true and "F" if it is false. The dialogue will be played twice.

25. 여자는 아침을 아직 못 먹었다. ＿＿＿＿

26. 여자는 아침을 먹었지만 또 먹을 것이다. ＿＿＿＿

27. 남자가 먹을 것을 사 올 것이다. ＿＿＿＿

28. 여자와 남자는 함께 나갈 것이다. ＿＿＿＿

Section VI - Speaking Practice

A native speaker will read the dialogue from Section V line by line. Listen and repeat each sentence one by one. You can check out the dialogue in the Answer Key at the back of the book.

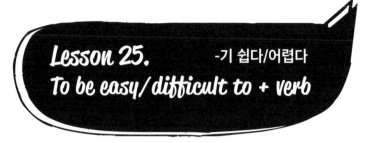

Lesson 25.
To be easy/difficult to + verb
-기 쉽다/어렵다

Section I - Vocabulary

Fill in the chart. The first one has been done for you.

	Verb	Meaning	Verb stem + -기	Meaning
1.	하다	to do	하기	doing
2.	잊다			
3.	먹다			
4.	사다			
5.	찾다			
6.	발음하다			
7.	만들다			
8.	사용하다			
9.	입다			

Section II - Fill in the Blank

Fill in the blanks by using the words from Section I and -기 쉽다/어렵다/좋다/불편하다/편리하다.

10. 중요하지 않은 일은 _____.

    = It is easy to forget things that are not important.

11. 김치는 _____.

    = Kimchi is difficult to make.

12. 다혜 씨 이름은 _____.

    = Dahye's name is difficult to pronounce.

13. 이렇게 넣으면 나중에 _____.

    = If you put it in like this, it is inconvenient to find it later.

14. 이 핸드폰은 _____.

    = This cellphone is convenient to use.

15. 간식으로 _____.

    = It is good to eat between meals.

16. 요즘에는 인터넷으로 선물 _____.

    = It is convenient to buy gifts online these days.

Section III - Complete the Dialogue

Complete each dialogue using the following structure and the words given in the parentheses. An example has been provided.

Structure:

-아/어/여서 -기 좋아요/어려워요.

= Because... it is good/difficult to [verb].

Example: (너무, 바쁘다, 만나다)

A: 동근 씨한테 물어보세요.

(= Ask Dong-geun.)

B: 동근 씨가 요즘 너무 바빠서 만나기 어려워요.

(= Because Dong-geun is so busy these days it's difficult to see him.)

17. (상자, 너무, 크다, 혼자, 들다)

　　A: 도와줄까요?

　　B: 네. ⁓⁓⁓⁓⁓⁓⁓⁓⁓⁓⁓⁓⁓⁓⁓⁓⁓⁓⁓⁓⁓⁓⁓ .

18. (눈, 많다, 오다, 빨리, 가다)

　　A: 몇 시까지 올 수 있어요?

　　B: 늦을 것 같아요. ⁓⁓⁓⁓⁓⁓⁓⁓⁓⁓⁓⁓⁓⁓⁓⁓⁓ .

19. (크다, 물건, 많이, 넣다)

　　A: 다혜 씨, 가방 진짜 크네요.

　　B: 네. 가방이 ⁓⁓⁓⁓⁓⁓⁓⁓⁓⁓⁓⁓⁓⁓⁓⁓⁓⁓⁓⁓ .

* 물건 = thing, stuff, object

20. (조용하다, -(으)ㄴ/는 편이다, 친해지다)

    A: 준배 씨랑 친해요?

    B: 아니요. 준배 씨는 _____.

> Structure:
>
> -(으)면 -기 쉬워요/불편해요. = If…, it is easy/inconvenient to [verb].
>
> Example: (치마, 길다, 춤추다)
>
> A: 이 치마 왜 안 입어요?
>
> (= Why do you not wear this skirt?)
>
> B: 치마가 길면 춤추기 불편해요.
>
> (= If a skirt is long, it is inconvenient to dance.)

21. (1번 출구, 나가다, 찾다)

    A: Talk To Me In Korean 사무실 어떻게 가요?

    B: 지하철 타고 가면 돼요. _____.

22. (너무, 크다, 쓰다)

    A: 어떤 지갑 살까요?

    B: 작은 지갑 사세요. _____.

23. (일찍, 자다, 일찍, 일어나다)

    A: 준배 씨, 어떻게 매일 아침 6시에 일어나요?

    B: _____.

24. (매일, 공부하지 않다, 배운 내용, 잊어버리다)

    A: 벌써 11시예요. 자고 내일 공부해요.

    B: 안 돼요. _____.

Section IV – Dictation

Listen to the sentences and fill in the blanks with the missing word or phrase. The sentences will be played twice.

25. 이건 어린이가 〰〰〰〰〰〰〰〰〰〰〰〰〰〰〰〰〰〰 .

26. Talk To Me In Korean 책은 〰〰〰〰〰〰〰〰〰〰〰〰〰 .

Section V – Listening Comprehension

27. Listen to the dialogue and list which statements are correct and which are incorrect. The dialogue will be played twice.

* 비빔밥 = bibimbap (mixed rice with assorted vegetables)
* 젓가락 = chopsticks

a. The woman eats bibimbap with chopsticks.

b. The man eats bibimbap with chopsticks.

c. The woman thinks bibimbap is easy to eat with chopsticks.

d. The man thinks bibimbap is easy to eat with chopsticks.

- Correct statements: 〰〰〰〰〰〰〰〰
- Incorrect statements: 〰〰〰〰〰〰〰〰

Section VI – Speaking Practice

A native speaker will read the dialogue from Section V line by line. Listen and repeat each sentence one by one. You can check out the dialogue in the Answer Key at the back of the book.

Section I - Vocabulary

Translate each word into English or your preferred language, then choose its antonym from the box and write it on the line provided. The first one has been done for you. (Translations in the Answer Key are given in English.)

덥다 적다 없다 가볍다 흐리다 두껍다 모르다

1. 얇다 (= to be thin) ↔ 두껍다

2. 맑다 (=) ↔ ~~~~~~~~~~~~~~~

3. 많다 (=) ↔ ~~~~~~~~~~~~~~~

4. 춥다 (=) ↔ ~~~~~~~~~~~~~~~

5. 무겁다 (=) ↔ ~~~~~~~~~~~~~~~

6. 있다 (=) ↔ ~~~~~~~~~~~~~~~

7. 알다 (=) ↔ ~~~~~~~~~~~~~~~

All words will be used in the following sections as well, so be sure to check your answers and commit each word to memory before you move on to the next section!

Section II - Complete the Dialogue

Complete each dialogue using -(으)ㄴ/ㄹ 줄 알았어요.

8. A: 비 오네. 현우 씨는 우산 가져왔네요? 비 ~~_____~~ ?

   B: 네. 아침에 날씨가 흐려서 비 ~~_____~~ .

9. A: 어? 석진 씨! 저 기다리고 있었어요?

   B: 네. 먼저 집에 ~~_____~~ ?

   A: 네. 아까 먼저 간다고 했잖아요.

10. A: 추운데 왜 이렇게 얇게 입고 왔어요?

    B: 오늘 별로 ~~_____~~ .

11. A: 지하철에 사람 진짜 많네요.

    B: 그러게요. 사람 별로 ~~_____~~ .

    * 그러게요. = I know. / Indeed.

12. A: 이렇게 무거운 걸 혼자 들려고 했어요?

    B: 네. 상자가 작아서 ~~_____~~ .

Section III - Comprehension

Using -(으)ㄴ/ㄹ 줄 몰랐어요, rewrite the sentences that you made in Section II.

13. A: 비 오네. 현우 씨는 우산 가져왔어요?

    B: 아니요. 오늘 비 ~~_____~~ .

14. A: 어? 석진 씨! 저 기다리고 있었어요?

   B: 네. 기다리고 _____?

   A: 네. 아까 먼저 간다고 했잖아요.

15. A: 추운데 왜 이렇게 얇게 입고 왔어요?

   B: 오늘 이렇게 _____.

16. A: 지하철에 사람 진짜 많네요.

   B: 그러게요. 저도 이렇게 사람이 _____.

17. A: 이렇게 무거운 걸 혼자 들려고 했어요?

   B: 네. 상자가 작아서 _____.

Section IV - Dictation

Listen to the sentences and fill in the blanks with the missing word or phrase. The sentences will be played twice.

18. 이렇게 _____.

19. _____?

Section V - Listening Comprehension

20. Listen to the dialogue and choose what the man is most likely to say right after the dialogue finishes. The dialogue will be played twice.

* 바뀌다 = to be changed

a. 아, 정말요? 예지 씨가 안 보낸 줄 몰랐어요.

b. 아, 정말요? 예지 씨한테 벌써 말 한 줄 알았어요.

c. 아, 정말요? 예지 씨가 보낸 줄 몰랐어요.

d. 아, 정말요? 예지 씨한테 아직 말 안 한 줄 알았어요.

Section VI - Speaking Practice

A native speaker will read the dialogue from Section V line by line.
Listen and repeat each sentence one by one. You can check out the
dialogue in the Answer Key at the back of the book.

Lesson 27.
Can, To be able to,
To know how to

Section I - Vocabulary

Choose the verb that can be used in all of the blanks.

1. • 스키(를) ＿＿＿＿＿＿ = to ski
   • 자전거(를) ＿＿＿＿＿＿ = to ride a bike
   • 스케이트(를) ＿＿＿＿＿＿ = to skate

   a. 보다   b. 읽다   c. 타다   d. 치다

2. • 테니스(를) ＿＿＿＿＿＿ = to play tennis
   • 볼링(을) ＿＿＿＿＿＿ = to bowl

   a. 타다   b. 치다   c. 놀다   d. 알다

3. • 피아노(를) ＿＿＿＿＿＿ = to play the piano
   • 기타(를) ＿＿＿＿＿＿ = to play the guitar

   a. 놀다   b. 알다   c. 타다   d. 치다

4. • 한글을 ＿＿＿＿＿＿ = to read Hangeul
   • 한자를 ＿＿＿＿＿＿ = to read Chinese characters

   a. 읽다   b. 쓰다   c. 듣다   d. 말하다

5. • 스페인어(를) _____ = to speak Spanish

   • 한국 요리(를) _____ = to cook Korean food

   a. 말하다   b. 만들다   c. 하다   d. 타다

6. • 빵(을) _____ = to make bread

   • 떡(을) _____ = to make rice cakes

   • 김치(를) _____ = to make kimchi

   a. 굽다   b. 튀기다   c. 자르다   d. 만들다

Section II – Complete the Dialogue

Complete each dialogue based on the corresponding drawing. Use the phrases from Section I – Vocabulary as well as -(으)ㄹ 줄 알다/모르다.

Ex) A: 테니스 칠 줄 알아요?
    B: 아니요. 칠 줄 몰라요.

7. A: _____ ?
   B: 네. 근데 잘 못 쳐요.

8. A: _____? 9. A: 승완 씨, _____?

   B: 아니요. 전혀 _____.   B: 아니요. _____.

                                          근데 스노보드는 잘 타요.

10. A: _____? 11. A: _____?

    B: 아니요. _____.   B: 네. _____.

       근데 배워 보고 싶어요.   근데 쓸 줄은 몰라요.

Section III - Comprehension

Complete each sentence by conjugating the word provided in the parentheses with one of the endings from the box.

> -(으)ㄹ 수 있어요/없어요   -(으)ㄹ 줄 알아요/몰라요
>
> -(으)ㄹ 줄 알았어요/몰랐어요

12. 현우 씨, 지금 잠깐 얘기 좀 _____? (하다)

13. 한국에서는 몇 살부터 _____? (운전하다)

14. 비밀이에요. 아무한테도 _____. (말하다)

15. 저희 딸은 아직 한글 _____. (쓰다)

16. 중국어 조금 _____. 중학교 때 배웠거든요. (하다)

17. 경화 씨, 왔어요? 바쁘다고 해서 못 _____. (오다)

18. A: 이 게임 어떻게 하는 거예요?

    B: 저도 _____. (하다)

Section IV - Dictation

Listen to the dialogues and fill in the blanks with the missing word or phrase.
The dialogues will be played twice

19. A: 소희 씨, _____?

    B: 네.

    A: 저 _____ 가르쳐 줄 수 있어요?

20. A: 저 엠마 씨 처음 봤을 때 긴장했어요.

    B: 왜요? 제가 승완 씨한테 _____?

    A: 네.

    B: 어렸을 때 _____, 지금은 다 잊어버렸어요.
    한국어밖에 못 해요.

Section V - Listening Comprehension

21. Listen to the dialogue and choose the correct statement. The dialogue will be played twice.

a. 여자는 떡을 만들 줄 안다.

b. 여자는 떡을 만드는 중이다.

c. 여자는 남자가 떡을 사 올 줄 몰랐다.

d. 여자는 떡 만들기가 어렵다고 생각한다.

Section VI - Speaking Practice

A native speaker will read the dialogue from Section V line by line. Listen and repeat each sentence one by one. You can check out the dialogue in the Answer Key at the back of the book.

Lesson 28.
It depends
-에 따라 달라요

Section I - Vocabulary

Answer each multiple choice question by circling the best answer.

1. 상황 means:

    a. time   b. always   c. weather   d. situation

2. Which of the following has the meaning of "time"?

    a. 해   b. 달   c. 때   d. 주말

3. Choose the word that best fits in the blank.

    • 작년 = last year

    • 올＿＿＿ = this year

    a. 해   b. 달   c. 때   d. 년

4. Choose the word that best fits in the blank.

    • 나라: 한국, 미국, 인도, 스페인

    • ＿＿＿＿＿: 봄, 여름, 가을, 겨울

    a. 나이   b. 학교   c. 가게   d. 계절

5. Read the sentence that describes the drawing below, and then choose the meaning of the underlined section.

• 두 사람은 머리 길이가 달라요.

a. length
b. color
c. weight
d. size

6. Read the sentence that describes the drawing below, and then choose the word that best fits in the blank.

• 크기는 같은데, _____ 는 달라요.

a. 길이
b. 색깔
c. 무게
d. 수박

Did you answer all the questions? All words will be used in the following sections as well, so be sure to check your answers before you move on to the next section and commit each word to memory!

Section II - Comprehension

7. Do these two sentences have the same meaning?

• 누구한테 이야기하는지에 따라서 달라요.
• 누구한테 이야기하느냐에 따라서 달라요.

a. Yes   b. No

8. Without changing the meaning of the sentence, change the underlined section to a three-syllable word.

  • 상황에 <u>따라</u> 달라요.

    Answer: _____

9. Do these sentences both mean, "It depends on the person"?

  • 사람에 따라 달라요.

  • 사람마다 달라요.

    a. Yes   b. No

10. Write one word that can fit in all of the blanks.

  • 날 _____ = every day
  • 주말 _____ = every weekend
  • 달 _____ = every month
  • 해 _____ = every year

    Answer: _____

11. Can "해마다 달라요" have both of the meanings below?

  • It depends on the year.
  • It changes every year.

    a. Yes   b. No

Section III - Complete the Dialogue

Complete the dialogues by choosing the appropriate expression from each box and conjugating it.

12.

언제 가다	-에 따라 다르다
누구한테 가다	-마다 다르다

A: 회사에서 집까지 차로 얼마나 걸려요?

B: ~~_____~~. 보통 20분밖에 안 걸리는데, 금요일에는 한 시간 걸려요.

13.

달	-에 따라 다르다
해	-마다 다르다

A: 지나 씨 생일이 오늘이라고요? 8월 9일 아니에요?

B: 아, 저는 생일을 음력으로 계산해서 ~~_____~~ 져요.

* 음력 = lunar calendar

14.

길이	-에 따라 다르다
무게	-마다 다르다

A: 책 주문하려고 하는데, 배송비가 얼마예요?   * 배송비 = shipping fee

B: 배송비는 ~~_____~~.
무거울수록 비싸요.

15.

| 사람 | -에 따라 다르다 |
| 직업 | -마다 다르다 |

A: 운전 배우고 싶은데, 얼마나 걸릴까요?

B: 음... ＿＿＿＿＿＿＿＿＿＿＿ 것 같아요. 제 친구 중의 한 명은 정말 빨리
배웠는데, 다른 친구는 정말 오래 걸렸어요.

16.

| 나라 | -에 따라 다르다 |
| 계절 | -마다 다르다 |

A: 예지 씨는 보통 몇 시에 일어나요?

B: 음... ＿＿＿＿＿＿＿＿＿＿＿＿＿＿＿＿ 것 같아요.
여름에는 일찍 일어나고, 겨울에는 좀 늦게 일어나요.   * 여름 = summer

Section IV - Dictation

Listen to the sentences and fill in the blanks with the missing word or phrase.
The sentences will be played twice.

17. ＿＿＿＿＿＿＿＿＿＿＿＿＿ 달라요.

18. ＿＿＿＿＿＿＿＿＿＿＿＿＿ 달라요.

Section V - Listening Comprehension

True/False- Listen to the dialogue and decide if each statement is true or false. Write "T" if the statement is true and "F" if it is false. The dialogue will be played twice.

* 파마하다 = to get one's hair permed
* 단발머리 = bob, bobbed hair
* 기본 = basic

19. The man and the woman are both at a hair salon. ﹏﹏

20. The woman is having her hair permed. ﹏﹏

21. The cost of a perm depends on the length of the person's hair. ﹏﹏

22. The woman wants to have her hair bobbed. ﹏﹏

Section VI - Speaking Practice

A native speaker will read the dialogue from Section V line by line. Listen and repeat each sentence one by one. You can check out the dialogue in the Answer Key at the back of the book.

Lesson 29.
Sometimes I do this, but other times I do that.

어떨 때는 -(으)ㄴ/는데,
어떨 때는 -아/어/여요.

Section I - Vocabulary

Use a dictionary to determine the part of speech for each word, then define/translate it into English. All words are used in the following sections as well, so be sure to check your answers and commit each word to memory before you move on to the next section! The first one has been done for you.

1. 외롭다 = adjective / to be lonely

2. 불친절하다 =

3. 편하다 =

4. 확인하다 =

5. 친절하다 =

6. 한가하다 =

7. 메일 =

8. 지나다 =

Section II - Complete the Dialogue

Complete each of the dialogues using all the expressions in the parentheses and "어떨 때는 -(으)ㄴ/는데, 어떨 때는 -아/어/여요".

9. A: 혼자 사니까 좋아요?

= Do you like living by yourself?

B: _____.

(편하다, -아/어/여서, 좋다, 외롭다, -아/어/여서, 싫다)

= Sometimes I like it because it is comfortable, but other times, I don't like it because I feel lonely.

10. A: 아직도 머리가 아파요?

= Do you still have a headache?

B: _____.

(괜찮다, 많이, 아프다)

= At times it's okay, but other times, it hurts a lot.

11. A: 요즘 하고 있는 일 어때요?

= How's work these days?

B: _____.

(좋다, 그만두다, -고 싶다)

= Sometimes I like it, but other times, I want to quit.

12. A: 요즘도 바쁘세요?

= Are you still busy these days?

B: _____ .

(한가하다, 정말, 바쁘다)

= Sometimes I'm free, but other times, I'm really busy.

13. A: 제가 석진 씨한테 메일 보냈는데 확인을 안 하네요.

석진 씨는 _____ .

(메일, 바로, 확인하다, 일주일, 지나다, -아/어/여도, 확인 안 하다)

= I sent an email to Seokjin, but he hasn't checked it. Sometimes he checks his email right away, but other times, a week passes and he still hasn't checked it.

B: 그럴 때는 전화해 보는 게 좋아요.

= In that case, you'd better call him.

14. A: 준배 씨는 친절해요, 불친절해요?

= Is Joonbae nice or not nice?

B: 준배 씨는 _____ .

(불친절하다, 정말, 친절하다)

= Sometimes he's not nice, but other times, he's very nice.

Section III - Reading Comprehension

Read the following letter and answer the questions.

예지 씨에게

예지 씨, 저 캐시예요.

생일을 진심으로 축하해요. 예지 씨가 많이 보고 싶어요. 한국에 있을 때 저를 많이 도와줘서 정말 고마웠어요. 예지 씨는 어떨 때는 귀여운 동생 같았는데, 어떨 때는 언니 같았어요.

저는 요즘 한국어 공부를 열심히 하고 있어요. 한국어 공부는 _____ ㉠ _____. 특히 띄어쓰기가 가장 어려워요. 같은 표현이어도 어떨 때는 _____ ㉡ _____ 데, 어떨 때는 _____ ㉢ _____ 서 헷갈려요. 그래도 열심히 공부하면 쉬워지겠죠?

그럼 7월에 한국에서 만나요. 생일을 다시 한번 축하해요.

20XX년 11월 20일

캐시

Vocabulary
-에게 = to / 특히 = especially / 헷갈리다 = to be confusing

---

15. Choose the correct English translation of the sentence, "어떨 때는 귀여운 동생 같았는데, 어떨 때는 언니 같았어요."

   a. Sometimes you were like a nice younger sister, but other times, you were like an older sister.

b. Sometimes you were like a nice older sister, but other times, you were like a younger sister.

c. Sometimes you were like a cute younger sister, but other times, you were like an older sister.

d. Sometimes you were like a cute older sister, but other times, you were like a younger sister.

16. Choose the sentence that best fits in the blank ㉠.

a. 어떨 때는 하는데, 어떨 때는 안 해요.

b. 어떨 때는 재미있는데, 어떨 때는 어려워서 재미있어요.

c. 어떨 때는 하는데, 어떨 때는 어려워서 재미없어요.

d. 어떨 때는 재미있는데, 어떨 때는 어려워서 재미없어요.

17. Fill in the blanks using 띄어 쓰다 and 붙여 쓰다.

같은 표현이어도 어떨 때는 _____㉡_____ 데,
어떨 때는 _____㉢_____ 서 헷갈려요.

㉡ _____

㉢ _____

18. Choose the correct statement according to the letter.

a. Cassie has plans to visit Korea again.

b. Yeji and Cassie are going to have a birthday party together.

c. Cassie learned Korean from Yeji.

d. From now on, Cassie is not going to study about spacing.

Section IV - Dictation

Listen to the sentences and fill in the blanks with the missing word or phrase. The sentences will be played twice.

19. _____?

20. 어떨 때는 운동하는 _____, 어떨 때는 운동하고 _____.

Section V - Listening Comprehension

21. Listen to the dialogue and choose what you can learn from it. The dialogue will be played twice.

* (코를) 골다 = to snore

a. The man snores heavily every night.

b. The man snores sometimes.

c. The woman sometimes does not snore.

d. The woman does not snore at all.

Section VI - Speaking Practice

A native speaker will read the dialogue from Section V line by line. Listen and repeat each sentence one by one. You can check out the dialogue in the Answer Key at the back of the book.

Lesson 30.
Sentence Building Drill #8

Section I - Vocabulary

Complete the multiple choice questions by circling the best answer.

1. The Korean word for "(for) a long time" is:

   a. 바로   b. 오래   c. 거의   d. none of these

2. 엄마를 _____ = to help mom

   a. 도움주다   b. 도움보다
   c. 도와주다   d. 도와보다

3. Choose the words that can fit in the blanks.

   - 수업을 _____ ㉠ _____ = to start school/a class
   - 시험이 _____ ㉡ _____ = the test is over

   a. ㉠ 끝나다 ㉡ 시작하다   b. ㉠ 시작하다 ㉡ 끝나다
   c. ㉠ 끝내다 ㉡ 시작되다   d. ㉠ 시작되다 ㉡ 끝내다

4. Choose the pair that are antonyms.

   a. 걸리다 ↔ 고르다   b. 좋아하다 ↔ 좋다
   c. 만들다 ↔ 있다   d. 복잡하다 ↔ 간단하다

5. The correct translation of the Korean word **일어나다** is:

    a. to get up   b. to get in

    c. to get on   d. to get off

6. The correct translation of the Korean word **고르다** is:

    a. to catch   b. to take

    c. to choose   d. to bring

Section II - Grammar Point Comprehension

Complete the sentences by conjugating the word provided in the parentheses with the ending from the box that is most appropriate.

-(으)ㄹ 줄 알았어요   -기는 해요   -기 어려워요/쉬워요

7. 날씨가 _____. (춥다)

    = I thought the weather would be cold.

8. 책을 _____. (좋아하다)

    = I DO like books. (But...)

9. 여기에 _____. (있다)

    = I thought he/she would be here.

10. 많이 _____. (어렵다)

    = I thought it would be very difficult.

11. 이거 ﹏﹏﹏﹏﹏﹏﹏﹏﹏﹏﹏﹏﹏﹏﹏﹏﹏. (좋다)

= This is good. (But...)

12. 오래 ﹏﹏﹏﹏﹏﹏﹏﹏﹏﹏﹏﹏﹏﹏﹏﹏﹏. (걸리다)

= I thought it wouldn't take a long time.

13. 늦게 ﹏﹏﹏﹏﹏﹏﹏﹏﹏﹏﹏﹏﹏﹏﹏﹏﹏. (일어나다)

= I thought you would wake up late.

14. 다 예뻐서 ﹏﹏﹏﹏﹏﹏﹏﹏﹏﹏﹏﹏﹏﹏﹏. (고르다)

= It's hard to choose because everything is pretty.

15. 이거 혼자서 ﹏﹏﹏﹏﹏﹏﹏﹏﹏﹏﹏﹏﹏﹏. (만들다)

= This is difficult to make by oneself.

Section III - Sentence Building Practice

Complete the sentences below using the sentences from Section II and -(으)ㄴ/는데. Then translate them into your preferred language. (Translations in the Answer Key are given in English.) An example has been provided.

Ex)

많이 어려울 줄 알았는데, 생각보다 쉽네요.

= I thought it would be very difficult, but it's easier than I thought.

---

16. ﹏﹏﹏﹏﹏﹏﹏﹏﹏﹏﹏﹏﹏﹏﹏﹏﹏, 너무 비싸요.

=

17. _____, 생각보다 많이 기다려야 되네요.

    =

18. _____, 도와 드릴까요?

    =

19. _____, 생각보다 일찍 일어났네요.

    =

20. _____, 생각보다 따뜻하네요.

    =

21. _____, 소설만 읽는 편이에요.

    =

22. _____, 없네요. 어디 갔어요?

    =

23. _____, 꼭 하나만 골라야 돼요?

    =

    * 꼭 = surely, at any cost

Section IV - Dictation

Listen to the sentences and fill in the blanks with the missing word or phrase.
The sentences will be played twice.

24. _____, 저녁에 할 거예요.

25. _____, 생각보다 간단했어요.

Section V - Listening Comprehension

Listen to the dialogue and answer the following questions. The dialogue will be
played twice.

26. What did the man think the movie would be like before he watched it?

   a. He thought it would be boring.

   b. He thought it would be fun.

   c. He thought it would be childish.

   d. He thought it would be scary.

27. What did the man say about the movie after watching it?

   a. It was difficult to understand.

   b. It was easy to understand.

   c. It was too long.

   d. It was very childish.

Section VI - Speaking Practice

A native speaker will read the dialogue from Section V line by line.
Listen and repeat each sentence one by one. You can check out the
dialogue in the Answer Key at the back of the book.

Answer Key
for
TTMIK
Workbook
Level 6

Lesson 1

Section I - Vocabulary

1. 점심을 먹다 = to have lunch
2. 안으로 들어가다 = to go inside
3. 이렇게 하다 = to do it like this
4. 다른 사람한테 물어보다 = to ask other people
5. 약속이 있다 = to have an appointment
6. 다시 하다 = to do again
7. 밖에 앉다 = to sit outside
8. 내일 만나서 이야기하다 = to meet and talk about it tomorrow

Section II - Translation Practice

9. 내일 어때요?
10. 비빔밥 어때요?
11. 5시 어때요?
12. 이렇게 하는 거 어때요? (Depending on the context, you can also add a marker to 거 and say 이렇게 하는 게 어때요? or 이렇게 하는 건 어때요?)
13. 안으로 들어가는 거 어때요?
14. 다른 사람한테 물어보는 거 어때요?
15. 내일 만나서 이야기하는 거 어때요?

Section III - Comprehension

16. 비빔밥은 어때요
17. 5시는 어때요
18. 이렇게 하는 거는/건 어때요
19. 내일은 어때요
20. 안으로 들어가는 거는/건 어때요

Section IV - Dictation

21. 생일 선물로 카메라 어때?
    (= How about a camera as a birthday present?)
22. 이렇게 하는 게 어때요?
    (= How about doing it this way?)

Section V - Listening Comprehension

<Transcript>
A: 경화 씨, 점심 뭐 먹고 싶어요?
B: 비빔밥 어때요?
A: 비빔밥 좋아요. 아는 식당 있어요?

A: Kyung-hwa, what do you want for lunch?
B: How about bibimbap?
A: Bibimbap sounds good. Do you know of a place?

23. b   24. d

Section VI - Speaking Practice

A: 경화 씨, 점심 뭐 먹고 싶어요?
   [경화 씨, 점심 뭐 먹꼬 시퍼요?]
B: 비빔밥 어때요?
   [비빔빱 어때요?]
A: 비빔밥 좋아요.
   [비빔빱 조아요.]
   아는 식당 있어요?
   [아는 식땅 이써요?]

Lesson 2

Section I - Vocabulary

1. d   2. e   3. f   4. g
5. b   6. h   7. c   8. a

Section II - Comprehension

9. a   10. b   11. c   12. d   13. a

Section III - Writing Practice

14. 제 아이디어에 대해서 어떻게 생각해요?
15. 그 소문에 대해서 어떻게 생각해?
16. 물어보는 것에/거에 대해서 어떻게 생각하세요?
17. 회사 어떤 것 같아?
18. 이 옷 입고 가는 것/거 어떤 것 같아요?

19. 한국으로 유학 가는 것/거 어떤 것 같아요?

Section IV - Dictation

20. 어떻게 생각하세요?

    (= What do you think?)

21. 이 책 어떤 것 같아요?

    (= What do you think about this book?)

Section V - Listening Comprehension

<Transcript>

여자: 주연이 결혼식 때 이 옷 입고 갈까? 어떻게

    생각해?

남자: 너무 화려하지 않아?

여자: 그럼 이건 어떤 것 같아?

남자: 오! 그게 훨씬 낫다.

Woman: Should I wear this to Jooyeon's wedding?

        What do you think?

Man: Isn't it a bit too colorful?

Woman: Then, what do you think about this?

Man: Oh! That's much better.

22.

- Correct statements: b
- Incorrect statements: a, c, d

Section VI - Speaking Practice

여자: 주연이 결혼식 때 이 옷 입고 갈까?

    [주여니 결혼식 때 이오딥꼬 갈까?]

    어떻게 생각해?

    [어떠케 생가캐?]

남자: 너무 화려하지 않아?

    [너무 화려하지 아나?]

여자: 그럼 이건 어떤 것 같아?

    [그럼 이건 어떤 걷 가타?]

남자: 오! 그게 훨씬 낫다.

    [오! 그게 훨씬 낟따.]

Lesson 3

Section I - Vocabulary, Part 1

1. 가장　　2. 들　　3. 중　　4. 의　　5. 하나

Section II - Vocabulary, Part 2

6. 제가 좋아하는　　　　7. 친한

8. 인기 있는　　　　　　9. 카페

10. 방법　　　　　　　　11. 웹사이트

12. 제가 자주 오는　　　13. 빠른

14. 큰

Section III - Conjugation Practice

6a. 제가 가장 좋아하는 가수들 중의 한 명(or 한 사람)

    이에요.

7a. 가장 친한 친구들 중의 한 명(or 한 사람)이에요.

8a. 가장 인기 있는 영화들 중의 하나예요.

9a. 가장 괜찮은 카페 중의 한 곳이에요.

10a. 가장 좋은 방법 중의 하나(or 한 가지)예요.

11a. 가장 좋은 웹사이트 중의 하나(or 한 군데)예요.

12a. 가장 자주 오는 곳 중 하나(or 한 군데)예요.

13a. 가장 빠른 길 중 하나예요.

14a. 가장 큰 이유 중 하나(or 한 가지)예요.

* You can replace 가장 with 제일, of course.

Section IV - Dictation

15. 가장 큰 이유 중의 하나예요.

    (= It is one of the biggest reasons.)

16. 제가 제일 좋아하는 책 중 하나예요.

    (= It is one of my favorite books.)

Section V - Listening Comprehension

<Transcript>

남자: 저는 박사 과정 포기해야 할 것 같아요.

여자: 왜요?

남자: 여러 가지 이유가 있는데, 가장 큰 이유 중의 하

    나는 높은 등록금이에요.

Man: I think I have to give up on my PhD.

Woman: Why?

Man: There are many reasons, but one of the biggest reasons is the high tuition.

17. a

Section VI - Speaking Practice

남자: 저는 박사 과정 포기해야 할 것 같아요.

   [저는 박싸 과정 포기해야 할껀 가타요.]

여자: 왜요?

   [왜요?]

남자: 여러 가지 이유가 있는데, 가장 큰 이유 중의 하나
   는 높은 등록금이에요.

   [여러 가지 이유가 인는데 가장 큰 이유 중에 하나
   는 노픈 등녹끄미에요.]

Lesson 4

Section I - Vocabulary

1. 열   2. 나중에 전화할

3. 먼저 갈   4. 열어 볼

5. 닫을   6. 나갔다가 올

7. 기다려   8. 설명해

Section II - Conjugation Practice

1a. 창문 좀 열어도 돼요?

2a. 나중에 전화해도 돼요?

3a. 저 먼저 가도 괜찮아요?

4a. 이거 열어 봐도 괜찮아요?

5a. 창문 닫아도 될까요?

6a. 잠깐 나갔다가 와도 될까요?

7a. 조금만 기다려 주실래요?

8a. 한 번 더 설명해 주실래요?

Section III - Comprehension

9. 창문 좀 열어도 돼

10. 나중에 전화해도 돼

11. 조금만 기다려 줄래

12. 한 번 더 설명해 주시겠어요

13. 잠깐 나갔다가 와도 될까요

Section IV - Dictation

14. 내일 말해 줘도 괜찮아요?

   (= Do you mind if I tell you tomorrow?)

15. 여기 앉아도 될까요?

   (= Do you mind if I sit here?)

Section V - Listening Comprehension

<Transcript>

여자: 지금 빈 테이블이 없네요. 조금만 기다려 주시
   겠어요?

남자: 네. 잠깐 나갔다가 와도 될까요?

여자: 네. 그럼 여기 전화번호 적어 주세요. 빈자리 나
   면 전화 드릴게요.

Woman: We currently do not have any empty ta-
bles. Would you mind waiting just a bit?

Man: Sure. Do you mind if I go somewhere and
come back in a moment?

Woman: Okay. Please write your phone number
here. We will call you if a table opens up.

16. a   17. b

Section VI - Speaking Practice

여자: 지금 빈 테이블이 없네요.

   [지금 빈 테이브리 엄네요.]

   조금만 기다려 주시겠어요?

   [조금만 기다려 주시게써요?]

남자: 네. 잠깐 나갔다가 와도 될까요?

   [네. 잠깐 나갇따가 와도 될까요?]

여자: 네. 그럼 여기 전화번호 적어 주세요.

   [네. 그럼 여기 전화번호 저거 주세요.]

   빈자리 나면 전화 드릴게요.

   [빈자리 나면 전화 드릴께요.]

Lesson 5

Section I - Vocabulary

1. 찾
2. 회사에 가
3. 운동하
4. 요리하
5. 공부하
6. 밥 먹
7. 하
8. 일하
9. 숙제하

Section II - Conjugation Practice

1a. 열쇠를 찾고 있는 중이에요. or 열쇠를 찾는 중이에요.
2a. 회사에 가고 있는 중이에요. or 회사에 가는 중이에요.
3a. 운동하고 있는 중이에요. or 운동하는 중이에요.
4a. 요리하고 있는 중이에요. or 요리하는 중이에요.
5a. 공부하고 있는 중이었어요. or 공부하는 중이었어요.
6a. 밥 먹고 있는 중이었어요. or 밥 먹는 중이었어요.
7a. 뭐 하고 있는 중이었어요? or 뭐 하는 중이었어요?
8a. 일하고 있는 중일 거예요. or 일하는 중일 거예요.
9a. 숙제하고 있는 중이에요. or 숙제하는 중이에요.

Section III - Complete the Sentence

10. 회의하는 중인데, 나중에 전화해도 될까요?
    = I am in a meeting, do you mind if I call you later?
11. 아직 고르는 중인데, 조금만 기다려 줄래요?
    = I am still choosing, do you mind waiting for a bit?
12. 지금 공부하는 중인데, 음악 소리 좀 줄여 줄래요?
    = I am studying now, do you mind turning down the music?
13. 지금 운전하는 중인데, 문자 메시지로 보내 주시겠어요?
    = I am driving now, do you mind sending it to me via text message?
14. 가는 중인데, 좀 늦을 것 같으니까 먼저 시작하세요.
    = I am on my way, but I think I am going to be a little late, so please start first.

Section IV - Dictation

15. 뭐 하고 있는 중이었어?

(= What were you doing?)
16. 공부하는 중이잖아요.

(= Come on, I am studying!)

Section V - Listening Comprehension

\<Transcript\>
여자: 석진 씨, 집에 도착했어요?
남자: 아니요. 지금 다시 회사로 가는 중이에요.
여자: 네? 왜요?
남자: 지갑을 놓고 왔어요.

Woman: Seokjin, did you get home?
Man: No. I'm on my way back to the office.
Woman: What? Why?
Man: I left my wallet there.

17. c

Section VI - Speaking Practice

여자: 석진 씨, 집에 도착했어요?
    [석찐 씨, 지베 도차캐써요?]
남자: 아니요. 지금 다시 회사로 가는 중이에요.
    [아니요. 지금 다시 회사로 가는 중이에요.]
여자: 네? 왜요?
    [네? 왜요?]
남자: 지갑을 놓고 왔어요.
    [지가블 노코 와써요.]

Lesson 6

Section I - Vocabulary

1. teacher / 선생님 / 선생님
2. doctor / 의사 / 의사 선생님
3. professor / 교수 / 교수님
4. head of a company / 사장 / 사장님
5. head of the department (or manager) / 과장 / 과장님

6. section chief / 부장 / 부장님

7. dean or president of a college

/ 총장 / 총장님

Section II - Comprehension

8. 경화 님

9. 어머니

10. 아버님

11. 어머님

12. 누님

13. 저는 의사예요 or 저는 의사입니다

14. 고객님

15. a. 과장 b. 부장 c. 사장

Section III - Dictation

16. 선현우 님, 들어오세요.

(= Mr. Hyunwoo Sun, please come in.)

17. 고객님, 안녕하세요?

(= Hello, sir/ma'am.)

18. 교수님, 총장님께서 찾으세요.

(= Professor, the college president wants to see

you.)

Section IV - Listening Comprehension

\<Transcript\>

A: 선생님, 안녕하세요. 저 민송이 엄마예요.

B: 민송이 어머님, 안녕하세요.

A: 민송이가 감기에 걸려서 지금 병원이에요. 오늘 유

치원에 10시까지 가도 될까요?

B: 네, 괜찮아요. 이따 뵐게요.

A: Hello. I'm Minsong's mother.

B: Hello, ma'am.

A: Minsong has a cold, so we're at the doctor's

office. Would it be all right if we got to the

kindergarten by 10?

B: Yes, that's fine. See you later.

19. c

Section V - Speaking Practice

A: 선생님, 안녕하세요.

[선생님, 안녕하세요.]

저 민송이 엄마예요.

[저 민송이 엄마예요.]

B: 민송이 어머님, 안녕하세요.

[민송이 어머님, 안녕하세요.]

A: 민송이가 감기에 걸려서 지금 병원이에요.

[민송이가 감기에 걸려서 지금 병워니에요.]

오늘 유치원에 10시까지 가도 될까요?

[오늘 유치워네 열씨까지 가도 될까요?]

B: 네, 괜찮아요.

[네, 괜차나요.]

이따 뵐게요.

[이따 뵐께요.]

Lesson 7

Section I - Vocabulary

1. d

2. b * 늦게 is the adverb form of

늦다 (= to be late).

3. a

4. a

5. b

6. c

7. a, b, c, d, e

Section II - Complete the Dialogue

8. A: 다혜 씨, 미안해요. 저 지금 가는 중이에요. 빨리 갈

게요.

(= I'm sorry, Dahye. I'm on my way now. I'll get

there soon.)

B: 어차피 늦었으니까 오지 마세요.

(= You are already late, so don't come.)

9. A: 핸드폰 안 가져가요?

(= You are not taking your cell phone?)

B: 네. 어차피 아무한테도 연락 안 와요.

(= No. Nobody will call me anyway.)

10. A: 이렇게 좋은 옷을 버려요? 아깝다.

(= You are throwing away such nice clothes?

They are too good to throw away.)

  B: 어차피 작아져서 못 입어요.

    (= They got smaller, so I can't wear them
    anyway.)

11. A: 숙제하기 너무 싫어요.

    (= I really don't want to do my homework.)

  B: 어차피 해야 하는 일이니까 재미있게 해요.

    (= One way or another, you have to do it
    anyway, so [you'd better] try to have fun while
    doing it.)

12. A: 우리 내일 다시 만나서 하는 게 어때요?

    (= How about we meet again tomorrow and
    do it?)

  B: 그래요. 어차피 오늘 다 못 할 것 같네요.

    (= Okay. I don't think we can finish it today
    anyway.)

13. A: 제 책상 위에 커피 있었는데... 혹시 승완 씨가 버
    렸어요?

    (= There was coffee on my desk. Did you throw
    it away, Seung-wan?)

  B: 네. 마시려고 했어요? 미안해요.

    (= Yes. Were you going to drink it? Sorry.)

  A: 아니에요. 괜찮아요. 어차피 거의 다 마셔서 버리려
    고 했어요.

    (= No. It's okay. I was almost done, so I was
    going to throw it away anyway.)

Section III - Dictation

14. 어차피 못 해요.

  (= It is obvious I can't do it.)

15. 어차피 제가 할 수 있는 일이 아니에요.

  (= Even if I try, it is not something that I can do.)

Section IV - Listening Comprehension

  <Transcript>

  A: 석진 씨, 가방 안 가져가요?

  B: 아, 어차피 이따가 사무실에 다시 올 거예요.

  A: 아, 퇴근하기 전에 사무실 들를 거예요?

  B: 네.

A: Seokjin, you're not going to take your bag?

B: Oh, I'm going to come back to the office in a
   little bit anyway.

A: Oh, so you'll come back to the office before
   leaving work?

B: Yes.

16. d

17. 어차피 이따가 사무실에 다시 올 거니까. or
    어차피 퇴근하기 전에 사무실 들를 거니까.

Section V - Speaking Practice

  A: 석진 씨, 가방 안 가져가요?

    [석찐 씨, 가방 안 가져가요?]

  B: 아, 어차피 이따가 사무실에 다시 올 거예요.

    [아, 어차피 이따가 사무시레 다시 올 꺼예요.]

  A: 아, 퇴근하기 전에 사무실 들를 거예요?

    [아, 퇴근하기 저네 사무실 들를 꺼예요?]

  B: 네.

    [네.]

Lesson 8

Section I - Vocabulary

  1. to be right, to be correct

  2. to be over, to be finished

  3. to open

  4. to be big

  5. to exist, to have

  6. where

  7. book

  8. bookstore

  9. meaning

  10. to not know

Section II - Conjugation Practice

  11. 맞다 / 맞는지 / 맞았는지 / 맞을지

  12. 끝나다 / 끝나는지 / 끝났는지 / 끝날지

  13. 열다 / 여는지 / 열었는지 / 열지

14. 크다 / 큰지 / 컸는지 / 클지

15. 있다 / 있는지 / 있었는지 / 있을지

16. 어디이다 / 어디인지 / 어디였는지
    / 어딜지 or 어디일지

17. 책이다 / 책인지 / 책이었는지 / 책일지

18. 서점이다 / 서점인지 / 서점이었는지 / 서점일지

19. 뜻이다 / 뜻인지 / 뜻이었는지 / 뜻일지

20. 모르다 / 모르는지 / 몰랐는지 / 모를지

Section III - Translation Practice

21. 좋은지 잘 모르겠어요.

22. 여기가 맞는지 잘 모르겠어요.

23. (그 사람이/남자가) 누구인지 잘 모르겠어요.
    * 누구인지 is often shortened to 누군지.

24. 서점이 문을 열었는지 잘 모르겠어요.

25. 어디에서 사야 되는지/하는지 잘 모르겠어요.
    * 어디에서 is often shortened to 어디서.

26. 뭘 해야 될지/할지 잘 모르겠어요.
    * 뭘 is short for 뭐를.

27. 언제 끝날지 잘 모르겠어요.

Section IV - Fill in the Blank

28. 만날지 안 만날지

29. 갈지 안 갈지

30. 끝났는지 안 끝났는지

31. 열었는지 안 열었는지

32. 있는지 없는지

Section V - Dictation

33. 저도 이 식당 처음 와 봐서 <u>뭐가 맛있는지</u> 잘 모르겠
    어요.
    (= This is also my first time coming to this
    restaurant, so I'm not sure what is good.)

34. 현우 씨가 요즘 바빠서 <u>만날 수 있을지</u> 잘 모르겠어요.
    (= Hyunwoo is busy these days, so I'm not sure if I
    will be able to meet/see him.)

Section VI - Listening Comprehension

<Transcript>

A: 경화 씨, 요즘도 요가 열심히 다녀요?

B: 네.

A: 어때요? 요가 하니까 좋아요?

B: 솔직히 좋은지 잘 모르겠어요.

A: Kyung-hwa, are you still attending yoga?

B: Yes.

A: How is it? Is doing yoga good?

B: Honestly, I'm not sure if it's good.

35. F   36. F

37. F   38. T

Section VII - Speaking Practice

A: 경화 씨, 요즘도 요가 열심히 다녀요?
   [경화 씨, 요즘도 요가 열씸히 다녀요?]

B: 네.
   [네.]

A: 어때요?
   [어때요?]
   요가 하니까 좋아요?
   [요가 하니까 조아요?]

B: 솔직히 좋은지 잘 모르겠어요.
   [솔찌키 조은지 잘 모르게써요.]

Lesson 9

Section I - Vocabulary

1. b   2. a

3. a   4. b

5. a   6. b

7. a   8. b

Section II - Complete the Sentence

9. 백화점에 <u>가는 김에</u> 서점에도 잠깐 <u>들를까?</u>

   = While we are going to the department store, shall we stop by the bookstore briefly as well?

10. 그 책 <u>반납하는 김에</u> 이 책도 <u>반납해 주세요.</u>

    = While you are returning the book, please return this book, too.

11. 밖에 <u>나간 김에</u> 제 부탁 하나만 <u>들어주세요.</u>

    = While you are outside, please do me a favor.

12. 서울에 <u>온 김에</u> 석진 씨한테 연락해 볼까요?

    = While we are visiting Seoul, shall we try contacting Seokjin?

13. 시작한 김에 끝까지 해 보려고 해요!

    = Since I've started it anyway, I'm trying to do it until the end.

Section III - Complete the Dialogue

14. 가는 김에   15. 간 김에

16. 말이 나온 김에   17. 온 김에

18. 나온 김에   19. 파마하는 김에

20. 돌리는 김에

Section IV - Dictation

21. <u>부탁하는 김에</u> 하나만 더 할게요.

    (= While I am asking for a favor, let me ask for just one more thing.)

22. <u>도서관에 가는 김에</u> 이 책 좀 반납해 주세요.

    (= While you are going to the library, please return this book.)

Section V - Listening Comprehension

<Transcript>

여자: 태호야, 뭐 해?

남자: 응, 라면 끓여.

여자: Taeho, what are you doing?

남자: I'm making ramyeon.

23. d

Section VI - Speaking Practice

여자: 태호야, 뭐 해?

   [태호야, 뭐 해?]

남자: 응, 라면 끓여.

   [응, 라면 끄려.]

Lesson 10

Section I - Vocabulary

1. 친했   2. 자주

3. 통화해요   4. 이따가

5. 나중에   6. 들르

7. 가져가

Section II - Complete the Sentence

8. 저 지금 일하는 중이어서 전화 못 받아요.

   (= I'm in the middle of work, so I can't take the call.)

9. 주연 씨 지금 통화하는 중이에요.

   (= Jooyeon is on the phone right now.)

10. 어차피 지금 가도 늦을 것 같아요.

    (= Even if we leave now, I think we will be late anyway.)

11. 어차피 오늘 다 못 할 것 같아요.

    (= I don't think we can finish it today anyway.)

12. 저랑 <u>제일 친한 친구 중 한 명</u>이에요.

    (= He/she is one of my best friends.)

13. 여기가 제가 제일 자주 가는 카페 중 한 곳이에요.

    (= This is one of the cafés that I visit most often.)

Section III - Sentence Extension

14. 여기가 제가 제일 자주 가는 카페 중 한 곳인데, 같이 가 볼래요?

    (= This is one of the cafés that I visit most often. Do you want to go there with me?)

15. <u>저랑 제일 친한 친구 중 한 명인데,</u> 만나 볼래요?

    (= He/she is one of my best friends. Do you want to meet him/her?)

16. 어차피 지금 가도 늦을 것 같은데, 가지 말까요?

(= Even if we leave now, I think we will be late anyway. Shall we not go?)

17. 어차피 오늘 다 못 할 것 같은데, 내일 다시 만나서 할까요?

(= I don't think we can finish it today anyway. Shall we meet again tomorrow and do it?)

18. 저 지금 일하는 중이어서 전화 못 받으니까, 나중에 전화할게요.

(= I'm in the middle of work, so I can't take the call. I'll call you later.)

19. 주연 씨 지금 통화하는 중이니까, 이따가 전화하라고 할게요.

(= Jooyeon is on the phone right now, so I'll tell her later to call you back.)

Section IV - Dictation

20. 책 읽는 중이었어요.

(= I was [in the middle of] reading a book.)

21. 제가 제일 좋아하는 영화 중 하나인데, 같이 볼래요?

(= It's one of my favorite movies. Do you want to watch it with me?)

Section V - Listening Comprehension

<Transcript>

여자: 제가 제일 좋아하는 한국 과자예요. 먹어 볼래요?

남자: 지금 게임 하는 중이니까 이따가 먹어 볼게요.

여자: 무슨 게임 해요?

Woman: This is my favorite Korean snack. Do you want to try?

Man: I'm in the middle of a game, so I'll try it later.

Woman: What game are you playing?

22. a

Section VI - Speaking Practice

여자: 제가 제일 좋아하는 한국 과자예요.

[제가 제일 조아하는 한국 과자예요.]

먹어 볼래요?

[머거 볼래요?]

남자: 지금 게임 하는 중이니까 이따가 먹어 볼게요.

[지금 께임 하는 중이니까 이따가 머거 볼께요.]

여자: 무슨 게임 해요?

[무슨 께임 해요?]

Lesson 11

Section I - Vocabulary

1. d	2. h	3. f	4. a	5. b
6. c	7. i	8. e	9. g	

Section II - Writing Practice

10. 그러니까 제 말은 벌써 다 끝났다는 말이에요

11. 그러니까 제 말은 지난주에 이미 샀다는 말이에요

12. 그러니까 제 말은 경은 씨가 최고라는 말이에요

13. 그러니까 제 말은 주연 씨를 정말 사랑한다는 말이에요

14. 그러니까 제 말은 아직 고르는 중이라는 말이에요

Section III - Comprehension

15. O

16. X → 아이스크림이 먹고 싶다고요.

17. X → 제일 자주 가는 카페라고요.

18. O

19. O

20. X → 그러니까 제 말은 지금 아무것도 안 하고 있다는 말이에요.

Section IV - Dictation

21. 그러니까 이거 저 준다고요?

(= You mean, you are giving this to me?)

22. 그러니까 혼자 간다는 말이에요?

(= You mean, you are going alone?)

<Transcript>

남자: 이 운동화 어때요?

여자: 오! 제가 좋아하는 스타일이에요. 근데 색깔이 엄청 화려하네요.

남자: 그러니까 좋다는 말이에요, 싫다는 말이에요?

여자: 다른 색깔은 없어요?

Man: How are these sneakers?

Woman: Oh! I like that style. But the color is really bright.

Man: So does that mean you like them or dislike them?

Woman: Isn't there a different color?

23. b   24. d

Section VI - Speaking Practice

남자: 이 운동화 어때요?

　[이 운동화 어때요?]

여자: 오! 제가 좋아하는 스타일이에요.

　[오! 제가 조아하는 스타이리에요.]

　근데 색깔이 엄청 화려하네요.

　[근데 색까리 엄청 화려하네요.]

남자: 그러니까 좋다는 말이에요, 싫다는 말이에요?

　[그러니까 조타는 마리에요, 실타는 마리에요?]

여자: 다른 색깔은 없어요?

　[다른 색까른 업써요?]

Lesson 12

Section I - Vocabulary

1. a　　2. c　　3. b　　4. d　　5. a　　6. b

Section II - Comprehension

7. b　　8. d　　9. a　　10. c　　11. b

Section III - Complete the Dialogue

12. A: 무슨 말인지 알겠어요.

　　(= I know what you mean.)

　B: 다행이네요.

　　(= That's a relief.)

13. A: 다혜 씨, 이거 다혜 씨가 다 해야 돼요.

　　(= Dahye, you have to do all of this.)

　B: 무슨 소리예요? 제가 왜요?

　　(= What do you mean? Why me?)

14. A: 무슨 말인지 잘 모르겠어요.

　　(= I don't know what you're talking about.)

　B: 다시 설명할게요. 잘 들어 보세요.

　　(= I'll explain it again. Listen carefully.)

15. A: 그만둘 거라고요? 갑자기 무슨 소리예요?

　　(= You're going to quit? What do you mean, all of a sudden?)

　B: 갑자기 아니에요. 사실 오래전부터 생각하고 있었어요.

　　(= It's not sudden. Actually, I've been thinking about it for a long time.)

16. A: 카메라를 팔 거예요.

　　(= I'm going to sell my camera.)

　B: 무슨 말이에요? 카메라도 없잖아요.

　　(= What do you mean? You don't even have a camera!)

Section IV - Dictation

17. 무슨 말씀이세요?

　(= What do you mean?)

18. 무슨 말씀이신지 잘 모르겠습니다.

　(= I am not sure what you mean.)

Section V - Listening Comprehension

<Transcript>

여자: 석진 씨, 주연 씨 생일 선물 저랑 같이 할래요?

남자: 네? 무슨 말이에요? 주연 씨 생일 지난달이었잖아요.

여자: 아! 주연 씨 말고 경은 씨요.

Woman: Seokjin, shall we buy Jooyeon's birthday present together?

Man: Huh? What do you mean? Jooyeon's birthday was last month.

Woman: Ah! Not Jooyeon, Kyeong-eun.

19. a   20. d

Section VI - Speaking Practice

여자: 석진 씨, 주연 씨 생일 선물 저랑 같이 할래요?

[석찐 씨, 주연 씨 생일 선물 저랑 가치 할래요?]

남자: 네? 무슨 말이에요?

[네? 무슨 마리에요?]

주연 씨 생일 지난달이었잖아요.

[주연 씨 생일 지난다리얻짜나요.]

여자: 아! 주연 씨 말고 경은 씨요.

[아! 주연 씨 말고 경은 씨요.]

Lesson 13

Section I - Vocabulary

1. 과거   2. 통과   3. 과민 반응

4. 과대   5. 과식   6. 과소비

7. 과신   8. 간과   9. 과속

10. 과로   11. 과민   12. 과정

Section II - Comprehension

13. c   14. a   15. d   16. c   17. b

Section III - Complete the Dialogue

18. A: 어, 여기 학교 앞이에요. 과속하면 안 돼요.

(= Oh, we're in front of a school. You shouldn't speed.)

B: 그러네요! 알려 줘서 고마워요.

(= Oh, you're right! Thanks for letting me know.)

19. A: 여보세요? 잘 안 들려요.

(= Hello? I can't hear you well.)

B: 지금 터널 안이에요. 터널을 통과하고 다시 전화할게요.

(= I'm inside the tunnel now. I will call you back after passing through the tunnel.)

20. A: 오늘은 과거 시제를 배울 거예요.

(= Today, we're going to learn the past tense.)

B: 과거 시제는 어제 배웠어요. 오늘은 미래 시제를 공부해야 돼요.

(= We learned the past tense yesterday. We have to study the future tense today.)

21. A: 경화 씨, 어제 본 영화 재미있었어요?

(= Kyunghwa, did you enjoy the movie you watched yesterday?)

B: 아니요. 그 영화는 너무 과대평가된 것 같아요.

(= No, I didn't. I think the movie is too over-rated.)

22. A: 승완 씨, 배부르지 않아요?

(= Seung-wan, aren't you full?)

B: 배부른데, 너무 맛있어서 계속 들어가네요.

(= I'm full, but it's so good that I keep eating.)

A: 과식은 몸에 안 좋아요. 그만 먹어요.

(= Overeating is not good for you. Stop eating.)

Section IV - Dictation

23. 과민 반응 하지 마.

(= Don't overreact.)

24. 과로하지 마세요.

(= Don't work too hard.)

Section V - Listening Comprehension

<Transcript>

A: 와, 이것 좀 보세요.

B: 왜요?

A: 봉투가 이렇게 큰데, 과자가 이만큼밖에 안 들어 있어요.

B: 요즘 과대 포장 너무 심한 것 같아요.

A: Whoa, look at this.

B: What is it?

A: The bag is so big, but there's only this much inside.

B: I think excessive packaging is ridiculous these days.

25. b   26. a

Section VI - Speaking Practice

A: 와, 이것 좀 보세요.

[와, 이걸 좀 보세요.]

* If you say it fast, [이걸 좀] becomes [이걸쯤].

B: 왜요?

[왜요?]

A: 봉투가 이렇게 큰데, 과자가 이만큼밖에 안 들어 있어요.

[봉투가 이러케 큰데, 과자가 이만큼바께 안 드러 이써요.]

B: 요즘 과대 포장 너무 심한 것 같아요.

[요즘 과대 포장 너무 심한 건 가타요.]

Lesson 14

Section I - Vocabulary

1. 바람(을) 좀 쐬다 = to get some fresh air

2. 밖(에) 나오다 = to come outside

3. 소설(을) 읽다 = to read a novel

4. 선물(을) 사다 = to buy a present

5. 산책(을) 하다 = to take a walk

6. 옷(을) 보다 = to look for some clothes

7. 사진(을) 찍다 = to take some photos

8. 남산(에) 가다 = to go to Namsan

Section II - Writing Practice

9. 한국어 공부도 할 겸, 한국어로 된 소설을 읽을 거예요

10. 회의도 할 겸, 커피도 마실 겸, 카페에 갈 거예요

11. 책도 읽을 겸, 공부도 할 겸, 도서관에 갈 거예요

12. 운동도 할 겸, 좀 걸을 거예요

13. 맛있는 음식도 먹을 겸, 바다도 볼 겸, 부산에 갔어요

14. 선생님도 만날 겸, 학교에 갔어요

15. 옷도 볼 겸, 점심도 먹을 겸, 백화점에 왔어요

16. 같이 영화도 볼 겸, 이야기도 나눌 겸, 현우 씨를 만났어요

Section III - Complete the Dialogue

17. A: 도서관에서 공부할 거예요?

(= Are you going to study at the library?)

B: 네. 책도 읽을 겸, 공부도 할 겸, 도서관에 갈 거예요.

(= Yes. I'm going to go to the library to read books and also to study.)

18. A: 어제 학교 갔어요?

(= Did you go to school yesterday?)

B: 네. 선생님도 만날 겸, 학교에 갔어요.

(= Yes. I went to school to see my teacher as well.)

19. A: 예지 씨, 또 백화점이에요?

(= Yeji, are you at the department store again?)

B: 네. 옷도 볼 겸, 점심도 먹을 겸, 백화점에 왔어요.

(= Yes. I came to the department store to look for some clothes and also to have lunch.)

20. A: 어제 현우 씨 만났어요?

(= Did you meet Hyunwoo yesterday?)

B: 네. 같이 영화도 볼 겸, 이야기도 나눌 겸, 현우 씨를 만났어요.

(= Yes. I met Hyunwoo to watch a movie together and also to talk.)

21. A: 어떤 책 읽을 거예요?

(= What book are you going to read?)

B: 한국어 공부도 할 겸, 한국어로 된 소설을 읽을 거예요.

(= I'm going to read a novel written in Korean to study Korean as well.)

22. A: 휴가 때 어디 갔어요?

(= Where did you go on vacation?)

B: 맛있는 음식도 먹을 겸, 바다도 볼 겸, 부산에 갔어요.

(= I went to Busan to eat good food and also to see the sea.)

Section IV - Dictation

23. 주연 씨는 화가 겸 작곡가예요.

    (= Jooyeon is a painter and composer.)

24. A: 어제 남산에 갔어요?

    (= Did you go to Namsan yesterday?)

    B: 네. 사진도 찍을 겸 해서요.

    (= Yes. To take pictures as well.)

Section V - Listening Comprehension

<Transcript>

남자: 엄마, 뭐 살 거 있어요? 저 운전 연습도 할 겸 마
트 갔다 올게요.

여자: 그래? 그럼 계란이랑 식빵 좀 사 와. 나가는 김에
쓰레기도 버려 주면 더 좋고.

남자: 네. 갔다 올게요.

Man: Mom, do you need anything? I want to practice driving so I'm going to the store.

Woman: Really? Then buy some eggs and bread.
I'd appreciate it if you also took out the
trash while you're at it.

Man: Okay. I'll be back soon.

25. a   26. d

Section VI - Speaking Practice

남자: 엄마, 뭐 살 거 있어요?

    [엄마, 뭐 살 꺼 이써요?]

    저 운전 연습도 할 겸 마트 갔다 올게요.

    [저 운전년습또 할 껨 마트 갇따 올께요.]

여자: 그래?

    [그래?]

    그럼 계란이랑 식빵 좀 사 와.

    [그럼 계라니랑 식빵 좀 사 와.]

    나가는 김에 쓰레기도 버려 주면 더 좋고.

    [나가는 기메 쓰레기도 버려 주면 더 조코.]

남자: 네. 갔다 올게요.

    [네. 갇따 올께요.]

Lesson 15

Section I - Vocabulary

1. 자유   2. 부자

3. 우정   4. 사람의 마음

5. 삶   6. 꿈

7. 진정한 친구   8. 행복

Section II - Comprehension

9. 행복이라는 것은 → 행복이란

10. 부자라는 것은 → 부자란

11. 우정이라는 것은 → 우정이란

12. 사람의 마음이라는 것은 → 사람의 마음이란

13. 삶이라는 것은 → 삶이란

14. 꿈이라는 것은 → 꿈이란

15. 진정한 친구라는 것은 → 진정한 친구란

Section III - Fill in the Blank

16. 진정한 친구란 어려울 때 도와주는 친구예요.

    (= A true friend is a friend who helps [you] when
    things are difficult.)

17. 꿈이란 쉽게 이룰 수 없는 거예요.

    (= A dream is what you can't easily achieve.)

18. 우정이란 사랑의 다른 이름이에요.

    (= Friendship is another word for love.)

19. 부자란 돈이 많은 사람이라는 뜻이에요.

    (= What they call 부자 is a person who has a lot
    of money.)

20. A: 사람의 마음이란 알 수 없는 거예요.

    (= A person's mind/heart is what you can't
    read.)

    B: 아니에요. 저는 다혜 씨 마음을 다 알 수 있어요.

    (= No. I know what is in Dahye's heart.)

21. A: 너무 아픈데 출근해야 돼요.

    (= I'm so sick, but I have to go to work.)

    B: 삶이란 원래 그런 거예요. 쉽지 않아요.

    (= That's how life is. It's not easy.)

Section IV - Dictation

22. 자유라는 것은, 아무거나 마음대로 하는 것이 아니에요.

    (= Freedom doesn't mean doing whatever [you want to do] in any way you like.)

23. 사랑이란 쉽지 않아요.

    (= Love is not easy.)

Section V - Listening Comprehension

\<Transcript\>

A: 경화 씨, 요즘 피츠버그 파이어리츠 성적이 안 좋아서 어떡해요?

B: 진정한 팬이란 팀 성적이 안 좋을 때도 꾸준히 응원하는 팬이죠.

A: 오! 멋있어요.

A: Kyung-hwa, the Pittsburgh Pirates' scores aren't very good these days, so what are you going to do?

B: People who call themselves true fans are those who cheer on their team even when their scores are bad.

A: Oh! You're admirable.

24. b   25. 다혜

Section VI - Speaking Practice

A: 경화 씨, 요즘 피츠버그 파이어리츠 성적이 안 좋아서 어떡해요?

[경화 씨, 요즘 피츠버그 파이어리츠 성저기 안 조아서 어떠캐요?]

B: 진정한 팬이란 팀 성적이 안 좋을 때도 꾸준히 응원하는 팬이죠.

[진정한 패니란 팀 성저기 안 조을 때도 꾸준히 응원하는 패니조.]

A: 오! 멋있어요.

[오! 머시써요.]

Lesson 16

Section I - Vocabulary

1. f	2. d	3. g
4. e	5. c	6. h
7. b	8. a	9. i

Section II - Comprehension

10. d

11. b

12. c

13. 드시겠어요 (먹다 is not an honorific word, so you cannot use it with -시겠어요.)

14. 죽겠어요

Section III - Complete the Dialogue

15. A: 아야!

    (= Ouch!)

    B: 아프겠어요.

    (= That must hurt.)

16. A: 어떤 가방을 살까요?

    (= Which bag shall I buy?)

    B: 이게 좋겠어요.

    (= I think this one will be good.)

17. A: 지금 몇 시예요?

    (= What time is it now?)

    B: 9시 50분이에요. 빨리 해요. 늦겠어요.

    (= It's 9:50. Hurry up. I think we'll be late.)

18. A: 이 상자 진짜 크죠?

    (= This box is really big, right?)

    B: 네. 저도 들어가겠어요.

    (= Right. Even I would [be able to] fit in it.)

19. A: 이 사람 알아요?

    (= Do you know this person?)

    B: 잘 모르겠어요.

    (= I don't know them.)

20. A: 지금 통화할 수 있어요?

  (= Can you talk on the phone now?)

  B: 죄송합니다. 지금 회의 중인데, 한 시간 후에 다시 전화해 주시겠어요?

  (= I am sorry. I am in a meeting now. Would you please call me back in an hour?)

Section IV - Dictation

21. 제가 하겠습니다.

  (= I'll do it.)

22. 혼자서도 되겠어요?

  (= Do you think you could handle it on your own?)

Section V - Listening Comprehension

<Transcript>

남자: 요즘 야식을 너무 자주 먹었어요. 오늘부터 6시 이후에는 아무것도 안 먹겠어요.

여자: 6시 이후에는 아무것도 안 먹겠다고요? 진짜 힘 들겠다.

남자: 할 수 있어요.

Man: I've eaten late-night snacks too often recently. From today, I won't eat anything after 6.

Woman: You won't eat anything after 6? That sounds hard.

Man: I can do it.

23. c   24. d

Section VI - Speaking Practice

남자: 요즘 야식을 너무 자주 먹었어요.

  [요즘 야시글 너무 자주 머거써요.]

  오늘부터 6시 이후에는 아무것도 안 먹겠어요.

  [오늘부터 여섣 씨 이후에는 아무걷또 안 먹께써 요.]

여자: 6시 이후에는 아무것도 안 먹겠다고요?

  [여섣 씨 이후에는 아무걷또 안 먹껜따고요?]

  진짜 힘들겠다.

[진짜 힘들겓따.]

남자: 할 수 있어요.

  [할 쑤 이써요.]

Lesson 17

Section I - Vocabulary

1. 빌려주다	2. 계속
3. 좀	4. 아까
5. 끝내다	6. 방금
7. 필요	8. 이미

Section II - Conjugation Practice

9. 갔거든요	10. 만났거든요
11. 바쁘거든요	12. 늦었거든요
13. 됐거든요	14. 끝냈거든요

Section III - Reading Comprehension

15. 불렀거든 or 했거든	16. 샀거든
17. 했거든	18. 공연이거든
19. 없거든	

<Translation>

Hanguk University 2020
Graduation Concert

- When? December 11, 2020 (Fri.) - December 12, 2020 (Sat.)
- Where? Hanguk University Main Hall
- How much? 1,000 won (If you buy a pamphlet, entry is free.)
- What? 2020 Graduation Concert (Part 1: Dancing, Part 2: Singing)

	December 11	December 12
15:00	김예지, 선경화	김희주, 석다혜
19:00	김희주, 석다혜	김예지, 선경화

Hyunwoo: I went to see the Hanguk University Graduation Concert last night.

Kyeong-eun: Really? How was it?

Hyunwoo: They danced and also sang songs, so it was really fun.

Kyeong-eun: Oh, it must have been really fun. How much was it?

Hyunwoo: It was free because I bought a pamphlet.

Kyeong-eun: How much is it if you don't buy a pamphlet?

Hyunwoo: It's 1,000 won if you don't buy a pamphlet. Take 1,000 won if you're going to go.

Kyeong-eun: Okay. By the way, did you see Kyung-hwa as well?

Hyunwoo: No, because Kyung-hwa performed at 3 o'clock yesterday.

Kyeong-eun: Aha! Is Kyung-hwa performing at 3 o'clock tomorrow as well?

Hyunwoo: Tomorrow is the 13th, right? You won't be able to see Kyung-hwa's performance tomorrow because today is her last performance.

Kyeong-eun: Really?

Hyunwoo: Yeah. The performance at 7 o'clock today is the last one.

Kyeong-eun: Then, can you possibly lend me just 1,000 won? I don't have any money now.

Section IV - Dictation

20. 필요 없거든요!

(= I don't need it!)

21. A: 현우 씨, 이게 무슨 일이에요?

(= Hyunwoo, what is this all about?)

B: 저도 모르겠네요. 사실 저도 방금 왔거든요.

(= I don't know either because I also just got here, actually.)

Section V - Listening Comprehension

\<Transcript\>

여자: 오늘 주연 씨 표정이 안 좋네요.

남자: 주연 씨 몸살감기 걸렸거든요.

여자: 아, 진짜요? 주연 씨! 아프면 일찍 퇴근해도 돼요.

Woman: Jooyeon doesn't look too good today.

Man: It's because Jooyeon caught a bad cold.

Woman: Oh, really? Jooyeon, if you don't feel well, you can leave work early.

22.

- Correct statements: a
- Incorrect statements: b, c, d

Section VI - Speaking Practice

여자: 오늘 주연 씨 표정이 안 좋네요.

[오늘 주연 씨 표정이 안 존네요.]

남자: 주연 씨 몸살감기 걸렸거든요.

[주연 씨 몸살감기 걸련꺼든뇨.]

* 거든요 is technically pronounced [거드뇨], but most people pronounce it [거든뇨].

여자: 아, 진짜요?

[아, 진짜요?]

주연 씨! 아프면 일찍 퇴근해도 돼요.

[주연 씨! 아프면 일찍 퇴근해도 돼요.]

Lesson 18

Section I - Vocabulary

1. 케이크를 먹다 = to eat cake

2. 자전거를 타다 = to ride a bicycle

3. 문자를 보내다 = to send a text message

4. 지하철을 타다 = to take the subway

5. 춤을 추다 = to dance

6. 모자를 사다 = to buy a hat

7. 김밥을 먹다 = to eat gimbap

8. 친구를 만나다 = to meet a friend

Section II - Comprehension

9. A: 뭐 먹을 거예요?

   (= What are you going to eat?)

   B: 김밥이나 케이크를 먹을 거예요.

   (= I'm going to eat gimbap or cake.)

10. A: 어떻게 연락할 거예요?

    (= How are you going to contact him/her?)

    B: 전화를 하거나 (아니면) 문자를 보낼 거예요.

    (= I'm going to make a call or send a text message to him/her.)

    (전화하거나 [아니면] is also possible.)

11. A: 회사에 어떻게 가요?

    (= How do you get to work?)

    B: 버스나 지하철을 타고 가요.

    (= I take the bus or subway.)

12. A: 동근 씨, 장기 자랑에서 뭐 할 거예요?

    (= Dong-geun, what are you going to do for the talent show?)

    B: 노래를 부르거나 (아니면) 춤을 출 거예요.

    (= I'm going to sing a song or dance.)

    (노래를 하거나 [아니면] 춤을 is also possible.)

13. A: 뭐 살 거예요?

    (= What are you going to buy?)

    B: 가방이나 모자를 살 거예요.

    (= I'm going to buy a bag or a hat.)

14. A: 경화 씨, 배고프면 빵을 먹거나 (아니면) 커피를 좀 마셔요.

    (= Kyung-hwa, if you are hungry, have some bread or drink some coffee.)

    B: 고마워요. 커피를 좀 마실게요.

    (= Thanks. I'll drink some coffee.)

15. A: 주말에 뭐 할 거예요?

    (= What are you going to do on the weekend?)

    B: 공부를 하거나 (아니면) 책을 읽을 거예요.

    (= I'm going to study or read a book.)

    (공부하거나 [아니면] 책을 is also possible.)

Section III - Reading Comprehension

<Translation>

Yeji: Dahye, what are you going to do today?

Dahye: I'm going to study at home or at a cafe.

Yeji: Oh, really? How about tomorrow?

Dahye: Umm... I'm going to study tomorrow as well.

Yeji: Tomorrow as well? Get some rest. It's Sunday! Let's hang out.

Dahye: Okay. What shall we do?

Yeji: How about riding a bicycle or watching a movie?

Dahye: I don't know how to ride a bicycle. Let's watch a movie.

Yeji: Good. Then I'll get back to you this evening or tomorrow morning.

16. 자전거(를) 타거나 영화(를) 보거나 or 영화(를) 보거나 자전거(를) 타거나

17. 저녁이나 or 저녁 아니면

18. 아니면

19. c

Section IV - Dictation

20. 친구를 만나거나 아니면 집에 갈 거예요.

    (= I'm going to meet my friend or go home.)

21. 여기나 저기에 놓아 주세요.

    (= Please put it here or there.)

Section V - Listening Comprehension

<Transcript>

여자: 현우 씨, 현우 씨는 주말에 주로 뭐 해요?

남자: 집에서 밀린 청소 하거나 빨래해요.

여자: 밖에 잘 안 나가요?

남자: 가끔은 나가서 친구들도 만나죠. 아니면 자전거 타는 거 좋아해서 날씨 좋으면 자전거 타요.

Woman: Hyunwoo, what do you usually do on the weekend?

Man: I do the cleaning that I've put off, or I do laundry.

Woman: You don't go outside that often?

Man: Sometimes I go out and meet friends. Or, because I like to ride my bike, if the weather is nice I'll go for a bike ride.

22. c   23. c

Section VI - Speaking Practice

여자: 현우 씨, 현우 씨는 주말에 주로 뭐 해요?

[혀누 씨, 허누 씨는 주마레 주로 뭐 해요?]

남자: 집에서 밀린 청소 하거나 빨래해요.

[지베서 밀린 청소 하거나 빨래해요.]

여자: 밖에 잘 안 나가요?

[바께 자 란나가요?]

남자: 가끔은 나가서 친구들도 만나죠.

[가끄믄 나가서 친구들도 만나조.]

아니면 자전거 타는 거 좋아해서 날씨 좋으면 자전거 타요.

[아니면 자전거 타는 거 조아해서 날씨 조으면 자전거 타요.]

Lesson 19

Section I - Vocabulary

1. 깨끗하다 (= to be clean) ↔ 더럽다

2. 멀다 (= to be far) ↔ 가깝다

3. 춥다 (= to be cold) ↔ 덥다

4. 조용하다 (= to be quiet) ↔ 시끄럽다

5. 짧다 (= to be short) ↔ 길다

6. 어렵다 (= to be difficult) ↔ 쉽다

7. 많다 (= to be a lot) ↔ 적다

8. 다르다 (= to be different) ↔ 같다

9. 크다 (= to be big) ↔ 작다

10. 넓다 (= to be wide) ↔ 좁다

Section II - Comprehension

11. 날씨가 추워졌어요.

(= The weather has gotten cold.)

12. 프랑스어 공부가 어려워졌어요.

(= I am studying French, and it has gotten hard.)

13. 방이 깨끗해졌어요.

(= The room has become clean.)

14. 줄이 짧아졌어요.

(= The line has gotten short.)

15. 교실이 시끄러워졌어요.

(= The classroom has become noisy.)

16. 키가 커졌어요.

(= He/she has gotten tall.)

Section III - Complete the Dialogue

17. A: 회사가 멀어요?

(= Is your company far?)

B: 옛날에는 멀었어요. 지금은 이사해서 가까워졌어요.

(= It was far before. Now that I've moved, it's become close.)

18. A: 살이 쪄서 옷이 작아졌어요.

(= I've gained weight, so my clothes have gotten small on me.)

B: 저랑 같이 운동할래요?

(= Do you want to work out with me?)

19. A: 다혜 씨, 아직도 추워요?

(= Dahye, are you still cold?)

B: 아니요. 이제 좀 따뜻해졌어요. 감사해요.

(= No. It's become a bit warmer now. Thanks.)

20. A: 캐시 씨, 한국어 발음이 정말 좋아졌어요.

(= Cassie, your Korean pronunciation has gotten really good.)

B: 감사합니다. 매일매일 연습했어요.

(= Thank you. I practiced every day.)

21. A: 어, 갑자기 조용해졌어요.

(= Uh, it suddenly became quiet.)

B: 아이들이 자나 봐요.

(= The children seem to be sleeping.)

Section IV - Dictation

22. 한국으로 여행 오는 사람들이 <u>많아졌어요</u>.

   (= The [number of] people who come to Korea for tourism have increased.)

23. 아까 여기 있었는데 <u>없어졌어요</u>.

   (= It was here earlier, but it disappeared.)

Section V - Listening Comprehension

\<Transcript\>

남자: 우와! 사무실이 예전이랑 많이 달라졌네요?

여자: 네. 많이 좋아졌죠?

남자: 직원도 훨씬 많아졌네요?

여자: 네. 회사가 훨씬 커졌어요.

Man: Wow! The office has changed a lot from before.

Woman: Yeah. It's gotten a lot nicer, right?

Man: There are more employees, too.

Woman: Yes, the company has gotten much bigger.

24. a, d   25. c

Section VI - Speaking Practice

남자: 우와!

   [우와!]

   사무실이 예전이랑 많이 달라졌네요?

   [사무시리 예저니랑 마니 달라전네요?]

여자: 네. 많이 좋아졌죠?

   [네. 마니 조아젇쪼?]

남자: 직원도 훨씬 많아졌네요?

   [지권도 훨씬 마나전네요?]

여자: 네. 회사가 훨씬 커졌어요.

   [네. 회사가 훨씬 커저써요.]

Lesson 20

Section I - Vocabulary

경화: 우와, 이 가방 샀어요?

   (= Wow, you bought this bag?)

다혜: 네. 지난주에 ¹· 백화점으로 쇼핑 가서 샀어요.

   (= Yes. I went shopping at the department store last week and bought it.)

경화: 얼마였어요?

   (= How much was it?)

다혜: 200,000원이요.

   (= It was 200,000 won.)

경화: 우와, 진짜 비싸네요! 제가 인터넷에서 본 ²· <u>가격</u>은 150,000원이었어요.

   (= Wow, that's really expensive! The price that I saw on the internet was 150,000 won.)

다혜: 정말요?

   (= Really?)

경화: 네. 다음에는 인터넷으로 먼저 ³· <u>알아보고</u> 사세요.

   (= Yes. Check the internet first the next time you buy something.)

다혜: 저 그런 거 잘 못하는데, 혹시 경화 씨한테 ⁴· <u>부탁</u> 해도 돼요?

   (= I'm not really good at that kind of thing. Can I possibly ask you to do it for me?)

경화: 네. 그럼 다음에 뭐 살 때 저한테 ⁵· <u>문자</u> 보내세요.

   (= Yeah. In that case, send me a text message next time you buy something.)

다혜: 네. 고마워요. 사실 내일도 ⁶· <u>나가서</u> 쇼핑하려고 했는데... 혹시 시간 되면 저랑 같이 쇼핑 갈래요?

   (= Okay, thanks. Actually, I was planning to go out shopping tomorrow as well... Do you want to go shopping with me if you have time?)

Section II - Comprehension

7. 핸드폰 가격도 <u>알아볼 겸</u>, 홍대에 갔어요.

   = I went to Hongdae to check the cellphone prices as well (while I was doing something else).

8. 여기에서 기다리거나 아니면 나가서 커피 마시고 있을게요.

= I will either wait here or go out and drink coffee.

9. 그러니까 혼자 올 거라고요?

= You mean, you're going to come by yourself?

10. 공부도 할 겸, 친구도 만날 겸, 도서관에 갈 수도 있어요.

= I might go to the library so I can study as well as meet a friend while I am there.

11. 그러니까 언제 할 거라고요?

= So, you said you were going to do it when?

12. 석진 씨한테 부탁하거나 아니면 그냥 제가 해 볼게요.

= I will either ask Seokjin or just give it a try myself.

Section III - Complete the Dialogue

13. A: 어디에서 회의할까요?

(= Where shall we have a meeting?)

B: 커피도 마실 겸 카페에서 해요.

(= Let's meet at a cafe so we can drink coffee as well.)

14. A: 미안해요. 저도 잘 모르겠어요.

(= I'm sorry. I don't really know either.)

B: 아니에요. 괜찮아요. 두루 씨한테 물어보거나 아니면 인터넷으로 알아볼게요.

(= No worries. I will either ask Duru or check on the internet.)

15. A: 그러니까 다음 주에 프랑스에 갈 거라고요?

(= So, you mean you are leaving for France next week?)

B: 네. 늦게 말해서 미안해요. 가서 연락할게요.

(= Yes. Sorry for telling you so late. I will call you when I get there.)

16. A: 오후에 어디 갈 거예요?

(= Where are you going to go in the afternoon?)

B: 예지 씨 생일 선물도 살 겸 백화점에 갈 거예요.

(= I'm going to go to the department store and will buy a present for Yeji's birthday there as well.)

17. A: 그러니까 승완 씨 생일이 지난달이었다고요?

(= So, you mean Seung-wan's birthday was last month?)

B: 네. 승완 씨 생일은 2월 25일이었어요.

(= Yes. Seung-wan's birthday was February 25th.)

18. A: 오늘 저녁에 전화하거나 아니면 문자 보낼게요.

(= I'll either call you or text you this evening.)

B: 네. 기다릴게요. 저녁에 꼭 연락 주세요.

(= Okay, I'll wait. Please make sure to reach me in the evening.)

Section IV - Dictation

19. 인사도 할 겸 다시 올 수도 있어요.

(= I might come back again to say hi as well.)

20. 그러니까 누구하고 같이 갈 거라고요?

(= So, I mean, who did you say you were going to go with?)

Section V - Listening Comprehension

<Transcript>

남자: 한국 드라마 보는 거 좋아해요?

여자: 아니요. 마크 씨는 좋아해요?

남자: 네. 한국어 공부도 할 겸 자주 봐요. 그럼 캐시 씨는 한국어 공부 어떻게 해요?

여자: 저는 유튜브 영상 보거나 아니면 팟캐스트 많이 들어요.

Man: Do you like watching Korean dramas?

Woman: No. Do you?

Man: Yes. I often watch them so I can also learn Korean. So then how do you study Korean?

Woman: I watch YouTube videos or listen to lots of podcasts.

21. 한국어 공부도 할 겸

22. 유튜브 영상 보거나 아니면

Section VI - Speaking Practice

남자: 한국 드라마 보는 거 좋아해요?

[한국 드라마 보는 거 조아해요?]

여자: 아니요.

[아니요.]

마크 씨는 좋아해요?

[마크 씨는 조아해요?]

남자: 네. 한국어 공부도 할 겸 자주 봐요.

[네. 한구거 공부도 할껌 자주 봐요.]

그럼 캐시 씨는 한국어 공부 어떻게 해요?

[그럼 캐씨 씨는 한구거 공부 어떠케 해요?]

여자: 저는 유튜브 영상 보거나 아니면 팟캐스트 많이 들
어요.

[저는 유튜브 영상 보거나 아니면 팟캐스트 마니 드
러요.]

Lesson 21

Section I - Vocabulary

1. 쌓이다 = to be piled up

2. 풀리다 = to come untied

3. 잘리다 or 잘라지다 = to get cut

4. 먹히다 = to be eaten

5. 쫓기다 = to be chased

6. 잡히다 = to get caught

7. 안기다 = to be hugged (안겨지다 is also used, even
though it is grammatically incorrect.)

8. 닫히다 = to be closed

9. 보내지다 = to be sent

10. 놓이다 = to be put down (놓여지다 is also used,
even though it is grammatically incorrect.)

Section II - Fill in the Blank

11. 도둑이 경찰한테 쫓기고 있어요.

(= The thief is being chased by the police.)

12. 신발 끈이 풀렸어요.

(= The shoelaces are undone.)

(풀려 있어요 is also possible, which will be covered in Level 7 Lesson 24.)

13. 갑자기 문이 닫혔어요.

(= Suddenly the door closed.)

14. 밖에 눈이 많이 쌓였어요.

(= A lot of snow has piled up outside.)

(쌓여 있어요 is also possible.)

15. 실수로 문자가 보내졌어요.

(= The text message has been sent by mistake.)

16. 코끼리가 뱀한테 먹혔어요.

(= An elephant has been eaten by a snake.)

17. 강아지가 저한테 안겨서 잠들었어요.

(= The puppy fell asleep in my arms.)

(안긴 채로 is also possible, which will be covered
in Level 10 Lesson 8.)

Section III - Comprehension

18. 저한테도 기회가 주어졌어요.

= I've also been given a chance.

19. 모자, 쇼핑백에 담아 드릴까요?

= Shall I put the hat in a shopping bag?

20. 하늘을 나는 방법이 연구되고 있어요.

= How to fly in the sky is being researched.

21. 저 어제 지하철에서 사람들한테 밀려서 넘어졌어요.

= Yesterday I was pushed by people on the subway, so I fell down.

22. Talk To Me In Korean 웹사이트를 이용하는 사람들
이 많아지고 있어요.

= More and more people are using Talk To Me In
Korean website.

Section IV - Dictation

23. 열쇠 담긴 상자 못 봤어요?

(= You haven't seen the box with the keys in it?)

24. '이용하다'가 아니고 '이용되다'예요.

(= It's not 이용하다, but 이용되다.)

Section V - Listening Comprehension

<Transcript>

여자: 왜 이렇게 뛰어와요? 누구한테 쫓기고 있어요?

운동화 끈도 풀렸어요.

남자: 예지 씨가 급한 일이라고 빨리 오라고 했잖아요.

여자: 제가요?

Woman: Why did you run? Are you being chased
by someone? Your shoelaces came undone, too.

Man: You said it was urgent and to come quickly.

Woman: I did?

25. c

Section VI - Speaking Practice

여자: 왜 이렇게 뛰어와요?

[왜 이러케 뛰어와요?]

누구한테 쫓기고 있어요?

[누구한테 쫃끼고 이써요?]

운동화 끈도 풀렸어요.

[운동화 끈도 풀려써요.]

남자: 예지 씨가 급한 일이라고 빨리 오라고 했잖아요.

[예지 씨가 그판 니리라고 빨리 오라고 핸짜나요.]

여자: 제가요?

[제가요?]

Lesson 22

Section I - Vocabulary

1. 무인	2. 무명	3. 무공해
4. 무시	5. 무조건	6. 무료
7. 무책임	8. 무한	9. 무죄
10. 무사고	11. 무적	12. 무능력
13. 무관심		

Section II - Comprehension

14. b   15. a   16. d   17. c   18. d

Section III - Complete the Dialogue

19. A: 윤아 씨, 운전 잘해요?

(= Yoona, are you good at driving?)

B: 네. 저 10년째 무사고 운전 중이에요.

(= Yes. I've been driving for 10 years without
an accident.)

20. A: 경화 씨, 돈 냈어요?

(= Kyung-hwa, did you pay?)

B: 아니요. 이거 무료예요.

(= No, it's free.)

21. A: 편의점에 사람이 아무도 없네요?

(= There's no one in this convenience store?)

B: 여기 무인 편의점이에요.

(= This is an unmanned convenience store.)

22. A: 우와, 또 이겼어요?

(= Wow, did you guys win again?)

B: 그럼요! 저희 팀은 무적이에요.

(= Of course! My team is invincible.)

23. A: 씻지 않고 바로 먹어도 돼요?

(= You can eat it right away without washing it?)

B: 무공해 농산물은 바로 먹어도 괜찮아요.

(= You can eat organic produce right away.)

Section IV - Dictation

24. 주연 씨는 먹는 것에 무관심해요.

(= Jooyeon is not interested in food.)

25. 무조건 다 좋아요.

(= Anything is good.)

Section V - Listening Comprehension

<Transcript>

여자: 이번 영화에서 어떤 역할을 맡았어요?

남자: 무명 배우 역할을 맡았어요.

여자: 승완 씨는 무명 시절에 어땠어요?

남자: 사람들이 저를 무시한다고 생각했어요. 그래서
촬영장 구석에서 많이 울었어요.

Woman: What role did you play in this movie?

Man: I played the part of the unknown actor.

Woman: How were your days as an unknown actor?

Man: I thought people were ignoring me. So I cried a lot on set in the corner.

26. b   27. c

Section VI - Speaking Practice

여자: 이번 영화에서 어떤 역할을 맡았어요?

[이번 영화에서 어떤 여카를 마타써요?]

남자: 무명 배우 역할을 맡았어요.

[무명 배우 여카를 마타써요.]

여자: 승완 씨는 무명 시절에 어땠어요?

[승완 씨는 무명 시저레 어때써요?]

남자: 사람들이 저를 무시한다고 생각했어요.

[사람드리 저를 무시한다고 생가캐써요.]

그래서 촬영장 구석에서 많이 울었어요.

[그래서 촤령장 구서게서 마니 우러써요.]

Lesson 23

Section I - Vocabulary

1. a   2. b   3. a, b
4. b   5. a   6. a
7. b   8. a   9. b

Section II - Fill in the Blank

10. 배터리가 없어서 핸드폰이 꺼졌어요.

(= Since the battery died, the phone turned off.)

11. 잘 안 들리는데, 좀 크게 말씀해 주시겠어요?

(= I can't hear you well. Could you speak up, please?)

12. 글씨가 작아서 잘 안 보이는데, 좀 크게 써 주세요.

(= The text is too small, so I can't see it well. Please write it big.)

13. 이해가 잘 안 되는데, 한 번 더 설명해 주시겠어요?

(= I can't understand it well. Could you explain it one more time, please?)

14. 석진 씨, 이 문제 너무 안 풀리는데 좀 도와주세요.

(= Seokjin, I can't really solve this question. Please help me.)

15. 어? 여기 카페였는데 식당으로 바뀌었네요.

(= Eh? There was a cafe here, but it's been changed to a restaurant.)

16. 프랑스어로 쓰인 책이네요. 현우 씨, 프랑스어도 할 수 있어요?

(= This book is written in French! Hyunwoo, can you speak French, too?)

Section III - Comprehension

17. 김밥 돼요?

= Do you have/serve kimbap?

18. 오늘 안에 돼요?

= Can you finish it today?

19. 영어가 안 돼서 걱정이에요.

= I'm worried because I can't speak English.

20. 이거 안 되는데 좀 도와주세요.

= I can't do this. Please help me.

21. 케이크를 예쁘게 만들고 싶은데 예쁘게 안 돼요.

= I want to make this cake into a pretty shape, but I can't make it pretty.

Section IV - Dictation

22. 불이 갑자기 켜졌어요.

(= The light turned on all of a sudden.)

23. 왜 그러는지 이해가 안 돼요.

(= I can't understand why he/she acts like that.)

Section V - Listening Comprehension

<Transcript>

여자: 어? 핸드폰이 갑자기 꺼졌어요.

남자: 배터리 없어요?

여자: 아니요. 고장 난 것 같아요. 아예 안 켜져요.

Woman: Huh? My phone died all of a sudden.

Man: Is the battery dead?

Woman: No. I think it's broken. It won't turn on at all.

24. b

여자: 어? 핸드폰이 갑자기 꺼졌어요.

[어? 핸드포니 갑짜기 꺼저써요.]

남자: 배터리 없어요?

[배터리 업써요?]

여자: 아니요.

[아니요.]

고장 난 것 같아요.

[고장 난 걷 가타요.]

아예 안 켜져요.

[아예 안 켜저요.]

Lesson 24

Section I - Vocabulary

1. 만나다

to meet

만나기는 만나요.

만나기는 만났어요.

만나기는 만날 거예요.

2. 헤어지다

to part ways

헤어지기는 헤어져요.

헤어지기는 헤어졌어요.

헤어지기는 헤어질 거예요.

3. 준비하다

to prepare

준비하기는 준비해요.

준비하기는 준비했어요.

준비하기는 준비할 거예요.

4. 도착하다

to arrive

도착하기는 도착해요.

도착하기는 도착했어요.

도착하기는 도착할 거예요.

5. 좋다

to be good

좋기는 좋아요.

좋기는 좋았어요.

좋기는 좋을 거예요.

6. 짜다

to be salty

짜기는 짜요.

짜기는 짰어요.

짜기는 짤 거예요.

7. 춥다

to be cold

춥기는 추워요.

춥기는 추웠어요.

춥기는 추울 거예요.

8. 맛있다

to be delicious

맛있기는 맛있어요.

맛있기는 맛있었어요.

맛있기는 맛있을 거예요.

Section II - Comprehension

9. 보기는 봤는데, 기억이 안 나요. / 보기는 했는데, 기억이 안 나요.

= I DID see it, but I don't remember.

10. 가기는 갔는데, 일찍 나왔어요. / 가기는 했는데, 일찍 나왔어요.

= I DID go there, but I left early.

11. 경은 씨를 만나기는 만났는데, 금방 헤어졌어요. / 경은 씨를 만나기는 했는데, 금방 헤어졌어요.

= I DID meet Kyeong-eun, but we parted soon after.

12. 읽기는 읽었는데, 아직도 무슨 말인지 잘 모르겠어요. / 읽기는 했는데, 아직도 무슨 말인지 잘 모르겠어요.

= I DID read it, but I don't really understand what it means.

13. 짜기는 짠데, 맛있어요. / 짜기는 한데, 맛있어요.

= It IS salty, but it tastes good.

14. 멀기는 먼데, 오늘 꼭 가야 돼요. / 멀기는 한데, 오늘 꼭 가야 돼요.

= It IS far, but I really have to go there today.

15. 아직 춥기는 추운데, 괜찮아요. / 아직 춥기는 한데,

괜찮아요.

= It IS still cold, but it's okay.

Section III - Complete the Dialogue

16. A: 어제 경은 씨 만났어요?

    (= Did you meet Kyeong-eun yesterday?)

    B: 경은 씨를 만나기는 만났는데, 금방 헤어졌어요. or 경은 씨를 만나기는 했는데, 금방 헤어졌어요.

17. A: 이 드라마 봤어요?

    (= Have you seen this drama?)

    B: 보기는 봤는데, 기억이 안 나요. or 보기는 했는데, 기억이 안 나요.

18. A: 김치찌개 맛이 어때요?

    (= How does the kimchi stew taste?)

    B: 짜기는 짠데, 맛있어요. or 짜기는 한데, 맛있어요.

19. A: 한국은 아직도 춥죠?

    (= It's still cold in Korea, right?)

    B: 아직 춥기는 추운데, 괜찮아요. or 아직 춥기는 한데, 괜찮아요.

20. A: 준배 씨, 이 책 읽었죠? 너무 어렵지 않았어요?

    (= Joonbae, you've read this book, right? It wasn't too difficult?)

    B: 네. 읽기는 읽었는데, 아직도 무슨 말인지 잘 모르겠어요. or 읽기는 했는데, 아직도 무슨 말인지 잘 모르겠어요.

21. A: 지금 지나 씨 집에 간다고요? 너무 멀지 않아요?

    (= You mean you are going to Jina's house now? Isn't it too far?)

    B: 멀기는 먼데, 오늘 꼭 가야 돼요. or 멀기는 한데, 오늘 꼭 가야 돼요.

22. A: 다혜 씨도 어제 졸업 파티 갔어요?

    (= Dahye, did you also go to the graduation party yesterday?)

    B: 가기는 갔는데, 일찍 나왔어요. or 가기는 했는데, 일찍 나왔어요.

Section IV - Dictation

23. 좋기는 좋은데, 너무 비싼 것 같아요.

    (= It IS good, but I think it's too expensive.)

24. 시간 맞춰서 도착하기는 했는데, 준비를 못 했어요.

    (= I DID manage to get there on time, but I couldn't prepare [before I left].)

Section V - Listening Comprehension

<Transcript>

남자: 경화 씨, 안녕하세요. 아침 먹었어요? 저 지금 나가서 먹을 거 사 오려고 하는데.

여자: 아침 먹기는 먹었는데, 또 먹을래요. 제 것도 부탁할게요.

남자: 네. 뭐 사 올까요?

Man: Hello, Kyung-hwa. Did you have breakfast? I was about to go out and bring back something to eat.

Woman: I did have breakfast, but I'll eat again. Get me something, too.

Man: Sure. What would you like?

25. F   26. T

27. T   28. F

Section VI - Speaking Practice

남자: 경화 씨, 안녕하세요.

    [경화 씨, 안녕하세요.]

    아침 먹었어요?

    [아침 머거써요?]

    저 지금 나가서 먹을 거 사 오려고 하는데.

    [저 지금 나가서 머글 꺼 사 오려고 하는데.]

여자: 아침 먹기는 먹었는데, 또 먹을래요.

    [아침 먹끼는 머건는데, 또 머글래요.]

    제 것도 부탁할게요.

    [제 껃또 부타칼께요.]

    * 제 것 is technically pronounced [제 걷], but most people pronounce it [제 껃].

남자: 네. 뭐 사 올까요?

    [네. 뭐 사 올까요?]

Lesson 25

Section I - Vocabulary

1. 하다 / to do / 하기 / doing
2. 잊다 / to forget / 잊기 / forgetting
3. 먹다 / to eat / 먹기 / eating
4. 사다 / to buy / 사기 / buying
5. 찾다 / to find / 찾기 / finding
6. 발음하다 / to pronounce /
   발음하기 / pronouncing
7. 만들다 / to make / 만들기 / making
8. 사용하다 / to use / 사용하기 / using
9. 입다 / to wear / 입기 / wearing

Section II - Fill in the Blank

10. 중요하지 않은 일은 잊기 쉬워요.
11. 김치는 만들기 어려워요.
12. 다혜 씨 이름은 발음하기 어려워요.
13. 이렇게 넣으면 나중에 찾기 불편해요.
14. 이 핸드폰은 사용하기 편리해요.
15. 간식으로 먹기 좋아요.
16. 요즘에는 인터넷으로 선물 사기 편리해요.

Section III - Complete the Dialogue

17. A: 도와줄까요?
    (= Do you need help?)
    B: 네. 상자가 너무 커서 혼자 들기 어려워요.
    (= Yes. The box is so big that it's difficult to lift
    by myself.)
18. A: 몇 시까지 올 수 있어요?
    (= What time can you make it here?)
    B: 늦을 것 같아요. 눈이 많이 와서 빨리 가기 어려워요.
    (= I think I'm going to be late. It snowed a lot,
    so it's difficult to get there quickly.)
19. A: 다혜 씨, 가방 진짜 크네요.
    (= Dahye, your bag is really big.)
    B: 네. 가방이 커서 물건을 많이 넣기 좋아요.
    (= Yes. My bag is big, so it's good for putting a
    lot of stuff in.)

20. A: 준배 씨랑 친해요?
    (= Are you close to Joonbae?)
    B: 아니요. 준배 씨는 조용한 편이어서 친해지기 어려워요.
    (= No. Joonbae is pretty quiet, so it's difficult to
    get close to him.)
21. A: TalkToMeInKorean 사무실 어떻게 가요?
    (= How do I get to the TalkToMeInKorean
    office?)
    B: 지하철 타고 가면 돼요. 1번 출구로 나가면 찾기 쉬워요.
    (= You can just take the subway. If you go out
    exit 1, it's easy to find it.)
22. A: 어떤 지갑 살까요?
    (= What kind of wallet shall I buy?)
    B: 작은 지갑 사세요. 너무 크면 쓰기 불편해요.
    (= Buy a small wallet. If it's too big, it's incon-
    venient to use.)
23. A: 준배 씨, 어떻게 매일 아침 6시에 일어나요?
    (= Joonbae, how do you manage to get up at 6
    o'clock every morning?)
    B: 일찍 자면 일찍 일어나기 쉬워요.
    (= If you go to bed early, it's easy to get up
    early.)
24. A: 벌써 11시예요. 자고 내일 공부해요.
    (= It's already 11 o'clock. Go to bed and study
    tomorrow.)
    B: 안 돼요. 매일 공부하지 않으면 배운 내용을 잊어버리기 쉬워요.
    (= No way. If you don't study every day, it's
    easy to forget what you've learned.)

Section IV - Dictation

25. 이건 어린이가 사용하기에도 쉬워요.
    (= This is easy for even a child to use.)
26. TalkToMeInKorean 책은 혼자 공부하기 좋아요.
    (= TalkToMeInKorean books are good for study-
    ing by yourself.)

<Transcript>

여자: 비빔밥을 젓가락으로 먹어요?

남자: 네.

여자: 왜요? 비빔밥은 젓가락으로 먹기 어렵잖아요.

남자: 아니에요. 전혀 어렵지 않아요.

Woman: You eat bibimbap with chopsticks?

Man: Yeah.

Woman: Why? It's hard to eat bibimbap with chopsticks.

Man: No, it's not hard at all.

27.
- Correct statements: b, d
- Incorrect statements: a, c

Section VI - Speaking Practice

여자: 비빔밥을 젓가락으로 먹어요?

[비빔빠블 젇까라그로 머거요?]

남자: 네.

[네.]

여자: 왜요?

[왜요?]

비빔밥은 젓가락으로 먹기 어렵잖아요.

[비빔빠븐 젇까라그로 먹끼 어렵짜나요.]

남자: 아니에요.

[아니에요.]

전혀 어렵지 않아요.

[전혀 어렵찌 아나요.]

Lesson 26

Section I - Vocabulary

1. 얇다 (= to be thin) ↔ 두껍다

2. 맑다 (= to be clear, to be sunny) ↔ 흐리다

3. 많다 (= to be a lot) ↔ 적다

4. 춥다 (= to be cold) ↔ 덥다

5. 무겁다 (= to be heavy) ↔ 가볍다

6. 있다 (= to exist, to have) ↔ 없다

7. 알다 (= to know) ↔ 모르다

Section II - Complete the Dialogue

8. A: 비 오네. 현우 씨는 우산 가져왔네요? 비 올 줄 알
   았어요?

   (= It's raining! Oh, you've brought an umbrella, Hyunwoo. You knew that it would rain?)

   B: 네. 아침에 날씨가 흐려서 비 올 줄 알았어요.

   (= Yes. Because it was cloudy in the morning, I knew that it would rain.)

9. A: 어? 석진 씨! 저 기다리고 있었어요?

   (= Eh? Seokjin! Have you been waiting for me?)

   B: 네. 먼저 집에 간 줄 알았어요?

   (= Yes. Did you think that I had gone home first?)

   A: 네. 아까 먼저 간다고 했잖아요.

   (= Yes. You said earlier that you would leave first.)

10. A: 추운데 왜 이렇게 얇게 입고 왔어요?

    (= It's cold. Why are you wearing such thin clothes?)

    B: 오늘 별로 안 추울 줄 알았어요.

    (= I thought it wouldn't be so cold today.)

11. A: 지하철에 사람 진짜 많네요.

    (= Wow, there are so many people on the subway.)

    B: 그러게요. 사람 별로 없을 줄 알았어요.

    (= Indeed. I thought there wouldn't be a lot of people.)

12. A: 이렇게 무거운 걸 혼자 들려고 했어요?

    (= Were you going to lift such a heavy thing by yourself?)

    B: 네. 상자가 작아서 가벼울 줄 알았어요.

    (= Yes. The box was small, so I thought it would be light.)

    (안 무거울 줄 알았어요 is also possible.)

Section III - Comprehension

13. A: 비 오네. 현우 씨는 우산 가져왔어요?

    (= It's raining! Hyunwoo, do you have an
    umbrella?)

    B: 아니요. 오늘 비 올 줄 몰랐어요.

    (= No. I didn't know it would rain today.)

14. A: 어? 석진 씨! 저 기다리고 있었어요?

    (= Eh? Seokjin! Have you been waiting for me?)

    B: 네. 기다리고 있을 줄 몰랐어요?

    (= Yes. You didn't know that I would be wait-
    ing?)

    A: 네. 아까 먼저 간다고 했잖아요.

    (= No, because you said earlier that you would
    leave first.)

15. A: 추운데 왜 이렇게 얇게 입고 왔어요?

    (= It's cold. Why are you wearing such thin
    clothes?)

    B: 오늘 이렇게 추울 줄 몰랐어요.

    (= I didn't know it would be this cold today.)

16. A: 지하철에 사람 진짜 많네요.

    (= Wow, there are so many people on the
    subway.)

    B: 그러게요. 저도 이렇게 사람이 많을 줄 몰랐어요.

    (= Indeed. I also didn't know that there would
    be this many people.)

17. A: 이렇게 무거운 걸 혼자 들려고 했어요?

    (= Were you going to lift such a heavy thing by
    yourself?)

    B: 네. 상자가 작아서 무거울 줄 몰랐어요.

    (= Yes. The box was small, so I didn't know that
    it would be heavy.)

Section IV - Dictation

18. 이렇게 비쌀 줄 몰랐어요.

    (= I didn't know it would be this expensive.)

19. 어디로 갈 줄 알았어요?

    (= Where did you think they would go?)

Section V - Listening Comprehension

<Transcript>

남자: 예지 씨, 제가 다혜 씨한테 약속 시간 바뀌었다고
방금 문자 보냈어요.

여자: 아! 제가 이미 보냈는데.

Man: Yeji, I just sent a message to Dahye that the
time has been changed.

Woman: Ah! I already sent her a message.

20. c

Section VI - Speaking Practice

남자: 예지 씨, 제가 다혜 씨한테 약속 시간 바뀌었다고
방금 문자 보냈어요.

[예지 씨, 제가 다혜 씨한테 약쏙 시간 바뀌얻따고
방금 문짜 보내써요.]

여자: 아! 제가 이미 보냈는데.

[아! 제가 이미 보낸는데.]

Lesson 27

Section I - Vocabulary

1. c   2. b   3. d   4. a   5. c   6. d

Section II - Complete the Dialogue

7. A: 기타 칠 줄 알아요?

    (= Do you know how to play the guitar?)

    B: 네. 근데 잘 못 쳐요.

    (= Yes, but I'm not very good at it.)

8. A: 스페인어 할 줄 알아요?

    (= Do you know how to speak Spanish?)

    B: 아니요. 전혀 할 줄 몰라요.

    (= No. I don't know at all.)

9. A: 승완 씨, 스키 탈 줄 알아요?

    (= Seung-wan, do you know how to ski?)

    B: 아니요. (스키) 탈 줄 몰라요. 근데 스노보드는 잘 타요.

(= No, I don't, but I'm good at snowboarding.)

10. A: 빵 만들 줄 알아요?

   (= Do you know how to make bread?)

   B: 아니요. (빵) 만들 줄 몰라요. 근데 배워 보고 싶어
   요. (= No, I don't, but I'd like to learn.)

11. A: 한자 읽을 줄 알아요?

   (= Do you know how to read Chinese characters?)

   B: 네. (한자) 읽을 줄 알아요. 근데 쓸 줄은 몰라요.

   (= Yes, I do, but I don't know how to write
   them.)

Section III - Comprehension

12. 현우 씨, 지금 잠깐 얘기 좀 할 수 있어요?

   (= Hyunwoo, can we talk for a second now?)

13. 한국에서는 몇 살부터 운전할 수 있어요?

   (= In Korea, from what age can you drive?)

14. 비밀이에요. 아무한테도 말할 수 없어요.

   (= It's a secret. I can't tell anyone.)

15. 저희 딸은 아직 한글 쓸 줄 몰라요.

   (= My daughter doesn't know how to write in
   Hangeul yet.)

16. 중국어 조금 할 줄 알아요 or 할 수 있어요. 중학교 때
   배웠거든요.

   (= I can speak a little Chinese because I learned in
   middle school.)

17. 경화 씨, 왔어요? 바쁘다고 해서 못 올 줄 알았어요.

   (= Oh, you're here, Kyung-hwa! Since you said
   you were busy, I thought you wouldn't be able to
   come.)

18. A: 이 게임 어떻게 하는 거예요?

   (= Do you know how to play this game?)

   B: 저도 할 줄 몰라요.

   (= I also don't know how to play it.)

Section IV - Dictation

19. A: 소희 씨, 테니스 칠 줄 알아요?

   (= Sohee, do you know how to play tennis?)

   B: 네.

   (= Yes.)

A: 저 테니스 칠 줄 모르는데 가르쳐 줄 수 있어요?

   (= I don't know how to play tennis. Can you

   teach me?)

20. A: 저 엠마 씨 처음 봤을 때 긴장했어요.

   (= I got nervous when I first saw you, Emma.)

   B: 왜요? 제가 승완 씨한테 프랑스어 할 줄 알았어요?

   (= Why? Did you think I would speak French to

   you?)

   A: 네.

   (= Yes.)

   B: 어렸을 때 프랑스어 할 줄 알았는데, 지금은 다 잊어
   버렸어요. 한국어밖에 못 해요.

   (= I knew how to speak French when I was

   young, but I've forgotten everything now. I can

   only speak Korean.)

Section V - Listening Comprehension

<Transcript>

여자: 제가 직접 만든 떡이에요. 한번 드셔 보세요.

남자: 네? 방금 직접 만들었다고 했어요? 소영 씨는 떡
   도 만들 줄 알아요?

여자: 네. 떡 만들기 어렵지 않아요.

Woman: I made this rice cake myself. Try it.

Man: Huh? Did you just say that you made it your-

   self? You know how to make rice cakes?

Woman: Yes. Rice cakes aren't hard to make.

21. a

Section VI - Speaking Practice

여자: 제가 직접 만든 떡이에요.

   [제가 직쩝 만든 떠기에요.]

   한번 드셔 보세요.

   [한번 드셔 보세요.]

남자: 네? 방금 직접 만들었다고 했어요?

   [네? 방금 직쩝 만드럳따고 해써요?]

   소영 씨는 떡도 만들 줄 알아요?

   [소영 씨는 떡또 만들 쭐 아라요?]

여자: 네. 떡 만들기 어렵지 않아요.

　　　[네. 떡 만들기 어렵찌 아나요.]

Lesson 28

Section I - Vocabulary

1. d　　2. c　　3. a　　4. d　　5. a　　6. c

Section II - Comprehension

7. a　　8. 따라서　　9. a　　10. 마다　　11. a

Section III - Complete the Dialogue

12. A: 회사에서 집까지 차로 얼마나 걸려요?

　　　(= How long does it take you to drive from the office to your house?)

　　B: 언제 가는지에 따라 달라요. 보통 20분밖에 안 걸리는데, 금요일에는 한 시간 걸려요.

　　　(= It depends on when you go. Usually, it only takes 20 minutes, but it takes an hour on Fridays.)

13. A: 지나 씨 생일이 오늘이라고요? 8월 9일 아니에요?

　　　(= You're saying that today is Jina's birthday? Isn't it on August 9th?)

　　B: 아, 저는 생일을 음력으로 계산해서 해마다 달라져요.

　　　(= Oh, I calculate my birthday based on the lunar calendar, so it's different every year.)

14. A: 책 주문하려고 하는데, 배송비가 얼마예요?

　　　(= I'm planning to order some books. How much is the shipping fee?)

　　B: 배송비는 무게에 따라 달라요. 무거울수록 비싸요.

　　　(= It depends on the weight. The heavier it is, the more expensive it is.)

15. A: 운전 배우고 싶은데, 얼마나 걸릴까요?

　　　(= I'd like to learn how to drive. How long do you think it will take?)

　　B: 음... 사람에 따라 다른 or 사람마다 다른 것 같아요. 제 친구 중의 한 명은 정말 빨리 배웠는데, 다른

친구는 정말 오래 걸렸어요.

　　　(= Umm... I think it depends on the person. One of my friends learned really fast, but it took my other friend a really long time.)

16. A: 예지 씨는 보통 몇 시에 일어나요?

　　　(= What time do you usually get up, Yeji?)

　　B: 음... 계절에 따라 다른 or 계절마다 다른 것 같아요. 여름에는 일찍 일어나고, 겨울에는 좀 늦게 일어나요.)

　　　(= Umm... I think it depends on the season. I get up early in the summer, and I get up a little late in the winter.)

Section IV - Dictation

17. 때에 따라 달라요.

　　　(= It depends on the time.)

18. 어디서 사는지에 따라 달라요.

　　　(= It depends on where you buy it.)

Section V - Listening Comprehension

<Transcript>

여자: 머리 파마하려고 하는데요. 얼마예요?

남자: 머리 길이에 따라 달라요. 단발머리니까 기본 가격으로 해 드릴게요.

Woman: I want to get a perm. How much is it?

Man: It depends on the length of your hair. Since your hair is bobbed, I can do it for the base price.

19. T　　20. F　　21. T　　22. F

Section VI - Speaking Practice

여자: 머리 파마하려고 하는데요.

　　　[머리 파마하려고 하는데요.]

　　　얼마예요?

　　　[얼마예요?]

남자: 머리 길이에 따라 달라요.

[머리 기리에 따라 달라요.]

단발머리니까 기본 가격으로 해 드릴게요.

[단발머리니까 기본 가겨그로 해 드릴께요.]

Lesson 29

Section I - Vocabulary

1. 외롭다: adjective / to be lonely
2. 불친절하다: adjective / to be unkind
3. 편하다: adjective / to be comfortable
4. 확인하다: verb / to check
5. 친절하다: adjective / to be kind
6. 한가하다: adjective / to be free
7. 메일: noun / email
8. 지나다: verb / to pass, to go by

Section II - Complete the Dialogue

9. A: 혼자 사니까 좋아요?

   B: 어떨 때는 편해서 좋은데, 어떨 때는 외로워서 싫어요.

10. A: 아직도 머리가 아파요?

    B: 어떨 때는 괜찮은데, 어떨 때는 많이 아파요.

11. A: 요즘 하고 있는 일 어때요?

    B: 어떨 때는 좋은데, 어떨 때는 그만두고 싶어요.

12. A: 요즘도 바쁘세요?

    B: 어떨 때는 한가한데, 어떨 때는 정말 바빠요.

13. A: 제가 석진 씨한테 메일 보냈는데 확인을 안 하네요. 석진 씨는 어떨 때는 메일을 바로 확인하는데, 어떨 때는 일주일이 지나도 확인(을) 안 해요.

    B: 그럴 때는 전화해 보는 게 좋아요.

14. A: 준배 씨는 친절해요, 불친절해요?

    B: 준배 씨는 어떨 때는 불친절한데 어떨 때는 정말 친절해요.

Section III - Reading Comprehension

<Translation>

To Yeji,

Yeji, this is Cassie.

A sincere happy birthday to you. I miss you a lot. Thank you so much for helping me out a lot while I was in Korea. Sometimes you were like a cute younger sister, but other times, you were like an older sister.

I'm studying Korean really hard these days. Sometimes studying Korean is fun, but other times, it's not fun because it's difficult. In particular, spacing between words is the most difficult. Even the same phrase is sometimes written with a space in the middle, but other times, it's written without a space, so it's confusing. Nevertheless, I believe it will get easier if I study hard, right?

Well then, I'll see you in July in Korea. Happy birthday once again.

November 20, 20XX

Cassie

15. c

16. d

17. ⓒ 띄어 쓰는, ⓒ 붙여 써 or ⓒ 붙여 쓰는, ⓒ 띄어 써

18. a

Section IV - Dictation

19. 어떨 때 제일 힘들어요?

    (= When do you [usually] have the hardest time?)

20. 어떨 때는 운동하는 게 재미있는데, 어떨 때는 운동하고 싶지 않아요.

    (= Sometimes working out is fun, but other times, I don't feel like exercising.)

Section V - Listening Comprehension

<Transcript>

남자: 안녕하세요, 의사 선생님. 제가 코를 너무 심하게 골아서 왔어요.

여자: 매일 밤 골아요?

남자: 아니요. 어떨 때는 심하게 고는데, 어떨 때는 안 골 때도 있어요.

Man: Hello, Doctor. I came because I have trouble with severe snoring.

Woman: Do you snore every night?

Man: No. Sometimes I snore heavily, but there are times when I don't snore at all.

21. b

Section VI - Speaking Practice

남자: 안녕하세요, 의사 선생님.

[안녕하세요, 의사 선생님.]

제가 코를 너무 심하게 골아서 왔어요.

[제가 코를 너무 심하게 고라서 와써요.]

여자: 매일 밤 골아요?

[매일빰 고라요?]

남자: 아니요.

[아니요.]

어떨 때는 심하게 고는데, 어떨 때는 안 골 때도 있어요.

[어떨 때는 심하게 고는데, 어떨 때는 안 골 때도 이써요.]

Lesson 30

Section I - Vocabulary

1. b   2. c   3. b   4. d   5. a   6. c

Section II - Grammar Point Comprehension

7. 날씨가 추울 줄 알았어요.

8. 책을 좋아하기는 해요.

9. 여기에 있을 줄 알았어요.

10. 많이 어려울 줄 알았어요.

11. 이거 좋기는 해요.

12. 오래 안 걸릴 줄 알았어요.

13. 늦게 일어날 줄 알았어요.

14. 다 예뻐서 고르기 어려워요.

15. 이거 혼자서 만들기 어려워요.

Section III - Sentence Building Practice

16. 이거 좋기는 한데, 너무 비싸요.

= This IS good, but it's too expensive.

17. 오래 안 걸릴 줄 알았는데, 생각보다 많이 기다려야 되네요.

= I thought it wouldn't take a long time, but we have to wait longer than I thought.

18. 이거 혼자서 만들기 어려운데, 도와 드릴까요?

= This is difficult to make by yourself. Do you want me to help?

19. 늦게 일어날 줄 알았는데, 생각보다 일찍 일어났네요.

= I thought you would wake up late, but you woke up earlier than I thought.

20. 날씨가 추울 줄 알았는데, 생각보다 따뜻하네요.

= I thought the weather would be cold, but it's warmer than I thought.

21. 책을 좋아하기는 하는데, 소설만 읽는 편이에요.

= I DO like books, but I tend to read novels only.

22. 여기에 있을 줄 알았는데, 없네요. 어디 갔어요?

= I thought he/she would be here, but he/she is not. Where is he/she?

23. 다 예뻐서 고르기 어려운데, 꼭 하나만 골라야 돼요?

= It's hard to choose because everything is pretty. Are you sure I can only choose one?

Section IV - Dictation

24. 오늘 하기는 할 건데, 저녁에 할 거예요.

(= I AM going to do it today, but I will do it in the evening.)

25. 복잡할 줄 알았는데, 생각보다 간단했어요.

(= I thought it would be complicated, but it was simpler than I thought.)

Section V - Listening Comprehension

<Transcript>
여자: 영화 재미있었어요?
남자: 재미있을 줄 알았는데 생각보다 재미없었어요.
여자: 왜요?
남자: 좀 이해하기 어려웠거든요.

Woman: Was the movie good?
Man: I thought it would be, but it wasn't as good as
     I thought.
Woman: Why?
Man: Because it was kind of difficult to understand.

26. b   27. a

Section VI - Speaking Practice
여자: 영화 재미있었어요?
    [영화 재미이써써요?]
남자: 재미있을 줄 알았는데 생각보다 재미없었어요.
    [재미이쓸쭐 아란는데 생각뽀다 재미업써써요.]
여자: 왜요?
    [왜요?]
남자: 좀 이해하기 어려웠거든요.
    [쫌 이해하기 어려월꺼든뇨.]
    * 좀 is technically pronounced [좀], but most
    people pronounce it [쫌].

Talk To Me In Korean Workbook